"Our love is as free as the wind. We cannot see it…
But we can feel it. If you want to see what marriage
looks like…Look at us!"—Zollie Harris

MIRROR IMAGE

Twin Flame relationships are on the telepathic level of a spiritual love, a telepathic love, a gentle ascending, of the Mind, Body, Soul, and Spirit. It is a Spiritual uniting in which you can see, feel, and hear the "other" as one spiritual merge. It is the ultimate Twin Flameship, which made its way into what the author calls a "direct zone into the heart of God".

MIRROR IMAGE

The Ascending Love Zone of Twin Flames

DAWN M. BUNCH

Archway Publishing books may be ordered through booksellers or by contacting:

Archway Publishing
1663 Liberty Drive
Bloomington, IN 47403
www.archwaypublishing.com
1 (888) 242-5904

Because of the dynamic nature of the Internet, any web addresses or links contained in this book may have changed since publication and may no longer be valid. The views expressed in this work are solely those of the author and do not necessarily reflect the views of the publisher, and the publisher hereby disclaims any responsibility for them.

Any people depicted in stock imagery provided by Thinkstock are models, and such images are being used for illustrative purposes only. Certain stock imagery © Thinkstock.

The author of this book does not dispense medical advice not prescribe the use of any technique as a form of treatment for physical or medical problems without the advice of a physician, either directly or indirectly. The intent of the author is only to offer information of a general nature to help you in your quest in this book for yourself, which is your constitutional right, as a self-publisher the author assumes no responsibility for your actions.

Design Concept by Dawn M. Bunch
Cover Photo by Curstan J. Bunch
Author Photo by Dawn M. Bunch
Illustrations by Dawn M. Bunch

ISBN: 978-1-4808-2972-5 (sc)
ISBN: 978-1-4808-2973-2 (e)

Library of Congress Control Number: 2016905672

Print information available on the last page.

Archway Publishing rev. date: 5/25/2016

DEDICATION

DEDICATION

I dedicate this vibrational offering of joy and peace to Twin Flameships, those who are vibrating toward their Twin Flame and to those who are attracting this information.

One must create a union of marriage with true self, as well as possessing those characteristics that you desire in your Twin Flame. Then you are ready to reunite with your Twin Flame, Divine Compliment. When you come full circle with your Twin Flame, you are destined for the path of ascension into this new fourth dimension.

We all are full recipients of a hurricane of grace...

Ah-shay! Ah-shay! Life is good!

GRATITUDE
GRATITUDE

I give gratitude to Father/Mother God creator of all things.

I give gratitude to the goodness of this universe.

I give gratitude the worthiness of our being.

I give gratitude that we are sparks of God.

I give gratitude on the reuniting of this Divine Twin Flameship.

I give gratitude that my Twin Flame is my 'Divine Compliment' in each other.

I give gratitude to our union of Oneness.

And so it is...

CONTENTS
CONTENTS

FOREWORD: HOW TWO BECOME ONE
FOREWORD: HOW TWO BECOME ONE

When I read this book, I felt a peaceful aura of divine inspiration on soul mate, marriage, and relationships. There is a new life; birthed deep within, realizing that divine unction, soul mate theory, is practically true, and that one can ignite the flame when meeting the one for whom each of us was created when we were taken out from his rib side by the creator.

The Twin Flame is a romantic paradox of a life journey of love that each one of us takes. Only by divine revelation can we see the very essence and light that has created such a wonderful, unique thing. This becomes a manifestation when we live our lives according to a God-centered point of view.

Dawn and Curtis' story reveals a divine way of connectedness that goes deeper, more spiritual, than could be expected in the natural. Devotion to the divine will cast while rejection and demotion seem to be what the dark side wants to place before us. This is like a Cinderella fairy-tale story. When you know who you are and whose you are, and have received a revelation of your God-given purpose in this universe, no downfalls will keep you from pursuing your passion in either a union, career, or divine path. When there is that moment of stillness in your spirit, there is a peace, that surpasses all understanding.

It comes directly from your creator, who Himself allows you to experience all these ups and downs, so at the end, you would give Him all the glory after you have gone through it.

At a certain point in time, when you discover that your life has more meaning than all the trials and struggles, you awaken to a divine uplifting, a paradigm shift which opens your inner thought to whom you were created to be. You can change the pattern of your present that the course of former life has led and controlled. *"Yes you can change any excuse pattern, no matter how long or pervasive the conditioning process has been." —Dr. Wayne W. Dyer*

The universe will always break open to release the sound of your voice and heart, so it can reach others who are also on a path you have already walked through. We must always remember that we are sojourners, and that we all we are solutions to others problems, and they will cross our path along the journey.

Dawn's writings, even other books she has created, has thus prepared a path to awaken consciousness, and a supernatural ambiguity that tends to cross the inner self of who we are and our purpose. Many times, we need a placebo to open us up.

Nevertheless, we are what we are; unless we believe we are who we will become. By overcoming those habits of excuses of past thoughts, both were able to cross each other's path and listen to each other's hearts, forgive all those who have caused hurt, and develop a new belief of consciousness, creating a new path that bond them and that is what makes the difference. Until you are divinely healed of those emotional tremors you can fully comprehend your values.

The hope within you will burst like a cocoon to expose new life and its meaning, setting you on a new adventure path of a greater journey for the universe. By applying the law of attraction, Dawn and Curtis have made their home a temple of kindness and love because they are on the same energy field, a spiritual path both have discovered on their quest for the divine to change the past.

The power of the tongue will bring either life or death. There is a higher power within us that has given us the authority to dominate, and the choice to speak our life into existence. There is always that moment of clarity and light inside of us to access that light and to give us divine guidance in whatever we do. This creates a pure energy field and an unlimited power we need to do divine works.

This I have seen in Dawn, practically in her environment how this has helped her transform so many situations that only could be accomplished in the supernatural. Dawn works with God and in doing so, she edges out the egos around her and this enables her to access her passion in writing and other things she has done in life, which amazes me.

Tapping into this energy has helped me so much in my own life, reconnecting me to the very essence of my being in some areas of my life that I took for granted and allowed my ego to control. At the end I found out that divine ordinance of God cannot be revealed when God is not in it. God cannot communicate with us if we disconnect from him when we behave in ways that separates us from Him. Hatred, revenge, fear, frustration, tension, worries, anger, and excuses will rob us from our divine connection and dim the flame in us and wrought darkness. After all that is who our source is, a forgiving God, which makes us like Him.

When Twin Flames burn in the same directional frequency, there is always a good and positive energy released, and the burning! When in any situation there is a wind set up to blow away the flame. The divine spirit who sees and knows it all, comes in and calms the wind and the cycle continues in good course on a higher frequency.

Within this spiritual union, both are attracted to what is in the heart, not lust. Twin Flames reveal a less risk-free union where love and forgiveness is the antidote to high tension and ego trip sentiments. This romantic journey mentored by the higher source of life and light is what every aspiring union should hope to have.

I know this book will serve as a mentor to those that are seeking their Twin Flame—their true love. It is an unfolding into a divine, long lasting, eternal union of divine oneness with God, the source of all creation.

"Every good and perfect gift is from above, coming down from the Father of lights, with whom there is no variation or shadow of turning." —James 1:17.

Reverend Hephzibah Ene Anderson Thomas
Healing Bond Sanctuary
Shreveport, LA

PART I:

INTRODUCTION
INTRODUCTION

The full vibration of oneness

Author:

Y ou are reading this book because you have some interest in what it has to say about **Twin Flames!** You, too, are seeking the answers on why your relationships are just not working out, what went wrong, and what to do after you have done everything to please them. You may even feel that you are the victim. In fact, you are not the victim, but you are the deliberate creator of your own reality.

"Oh that's easy for you to say dear author, you don't know what it's like having been in an abusive relationship for 25 years, with three kids, a dog, two cats and a gold fish and no cell phone. That's right, I'm pinned to the post, taking care of the kids, dog, cats and gold fish while I get my lickings because dinner was five minutes late with a slap, punch, kick and a kiss unable to call anyone to my rescue. Moreover, you say that I am not the victim! Screw you author! Oh and by the way author, what the heck is a Twin Flame and where is mine?"

Hey reader, before you go off on the fact that I don't know what I'm talking about or that I need to mind my own business, here are some questions that you may want to ask yourself. Who are you?

Why are you here? What is your purpose on this planet? Are you happy? Are you having fun? You have to know the answers before you can be with your "Twin Flame". Granted there are many relationships with good and bad experiences.

If it did not work out, then it just was not meant for them to be your twin flame. Do not take it personal; look at it as an experience that was part of your journey. It is said, that every relationship that you encounter prepares you for the ultimate relationship—the relationship with your Twin Flame.

In today's society, there is much discord in a lot of marriages and relationships. Such dis-harmony results in compromising conditions that result in failure. and you just do not understand why! Many homes are faced with an alarming rate of divorce, infidelity, violence, and abuse. Not only does it affect the emotional, mental, physical, and spiritual well-being, but also the ultimate affect is on your children.

Moreover, kids will often mimic what they are exposed too. Such discord leads to the many broken homes surrounded by the disharmony of one's mind, body, soul and spirit. And guess what? You grow up thinking and believing in these conditions and this is how it is supposed to be. This is not a discriminatory condition; it is a part of everyone's life's journey; it is what we were conditioned to believe, think and feel.

Contrary to popular belief, I decided to change my belief system! I say that to say this: I just refuse to believe, think, and feel that my relationships failed on the account of something we both did! No one is to blame! It just simply was not "meant to *be*". As the author and co-creator of this book, I welcome those who are attracting this Information. You are willing to be open and receptive yielding to the infinite possibilities that are everywhere present in its totality.

Now that you have gotten this far, you have willingly accepted the terms of this vibrational contract to read further. Upon the completion of this book and having made this tool applicable to your daily lives, you and your Twin Flame or significant other, will have met all the necessary requirements—to enter into Twin Flameship. Together, you will live a joyful, harmonious, and fulfilling life of oneness with God and each other.

Through recent research based on Twin Flameships, many Twin Flame couples were reunited during and after the 2012 Ascension. It revealed the vision of true divine eternal unconditional Twin Flame love. On December 20, 2012, people gave a lot of thought to the world ending. In fact, it was on that twenty-first day of the Winter Solstice that Ascension took place—purifying and crystallizing our planet.

My intent is to knock readers off their square of conventional thinking! I want this story to raise your awareness to a higher vibration. We are all radiant *beings* of light. On this journey, you will come to know that together, we are on the path of love through a planetary shift. The reuniting of Twin Flames throughout the global community draws us much closer. "When we act upon our intuitiveness of unconditional love, it binds us all into a collective good. Of course, that is just my opinion!"

The mere fact that I have a Twin Flame and never knew of it having met during the Summer Solstice on June 21, 2001. The amazing thing is that we share one soul. Today, as I reflect on our mirrored life experiences, it's as if we were in the "Twilight Zone". Rod Serling narrated an episode called "Mirror Image". That particular show validated my story as it relates to the very essence of our being. Our connection was for a sole purpose that prepared us for the beginning of our ascension on December 21, 2012.

Twin Flame unions are on the telepathic level of a spiritual love, a telepathic love, a gentle ascending of mind, body, soul, and spirit. We have merged spiritually as one! This sacred merging did not come through a public announcement of us just saying *I DO* and jumping the broom! It was a divine spiritual uniting in which we could see, feel, and hear each other...Our Twin Flameship made its way into what I call a "direct zone into the heart of God". We were joined together through divine order in such a way where things became evident that our union was indeed a significant part of the December 2012 Winter Solstice.

As I looked back on the series of events that happened in both our lives...Well—I find it astounding! As many of you will be in disbelief, only because you have a closed mind to the possibilities around you.

On page 5, the chart illustrates the 'mirrored' life experiences that my husband and I share, and have in common today.

'MIRRORED' LIFE EXPERIENCES

CURTIS	DAWN
DOB: August 4, 1955	DOB: August 31, 1965
Birth Age: 58	Birth Age: 48
S.S # Last two digits are same	S.S. # Last two digits are same
Curtis' middle name: Jerome	Uncles' name was: Jerome
Sons' middle name: Jerome	Cousins' middle name: Jerome
Mother Transitioned on: 12/24	Grandmother born: 12/24
Daughter born: 05/19	Our Daughter Born: 06/19
Daughter born: 09/20/1984	
Son born: 09/14	Daughter born: 09/14
Son born: 10/15	
Two Daughters last letter in first name: A	One Daughter last letter in first name: A
Lived in Delaware 1985	Lived in Delaware 1985
Separation and Divorce 2002	Separation and Divorce 2002
Professional Football	Professional Tennis
High School Colors: Purple& Gold	High School Colors: Purple & Gold
High School Mascot: Leopard	High School Mascot: Panther
Saw Dawn at Freeway Golf Course in June 2000 during the Summer Solstice	Saw Curtis at Freeway Golf Course in June 2001 during the Summer Solstice
Advocate Golfer	Advocate Golfer

Illustration Chart 1-1

Twin Flame Unions are essential in bringing the healing of separation into the full vibration of oneness. They are of the divine number 11:11. You will see a chart illustrating Curtis and Dawn's life experiences and their purpose here is of the divine 11:11 inside the infinity spectrum. Twin Flame Union is the ultimate balancing of the two primal forces of creation. As Twin Flames reunite, they become One.

Our daughter was born the month of June during the 2005 Summer Solstice. The second number of our age along with our daughter Curstan's age is always the same. The last digit in each of our birth year is five. The last two numbers in my husband and I social security numbers are the same. The illustration displayed is past and current mirrored experiences. It is evident that we share a divine connection in mind, body, soul, and spirit…Reuniting a split soul back to one.

> We all long for our true love, hoping for that connection with the ultimate mate to spend the rest of our lives in the physical and non-physical realm. The Twin Flame Union is not by a contract of marriage; they are eternally married within their very being that which no one can change.

THE FOUNDATION
THE FOUNDATION

We Are A Circle of Oneness ever Expanding

Today, we invite you to enter into our circle of oneness, our Twin Flameship. We welcome you into our hearts with a fullness of love, abundance, plentitude, peace, harmony, happiness, and well-being. In this moment, there is an unfolding taking place in your life right now!

As we partake on this wondrous journey together, allow this emergence of oneness to flow to you and through you. This creates a peaceful harmonious flow of Unconditional Love and Joy that is present everywhere in its totality. We give much gratitude and thanks to Father/Mother Earth always embracing and nurturing us with divine unconditional love…The true Essence of our Being, which connects and unifies ALL that IS.

We are ever expanding! Love is our nature; it is life! To become part of this ascension, you must be in connection with God Source in some infinitesimal but profound way.

Love Is Relating…It Knows No Full Stops

Love is the connection that simply holds the universe together. Love is eternal; it is unending. It is the absolute all-embracing acquiescence of what is—like a river always free-flowing. It is the honeymoon never ends!

Your Twin Flame Is Your Perfect Match

As I evoked the presence of God Source, I acknowledged the abundance of grace, love, and patience deeply rooted inside me. From what I understand today, all of my Charka's had connected to that sacred light of divinity centered well within my being. When I looked to that magnetic central sun in my heart, I knew that I was ready for my Twin Flame and so was he. Father/Mother God from the ocean of love connected us in a way that was of divine works, that originates from the same One Essence of creation.

We were a match spawned from perfection! The universe prepared us for our ascension to fulfill our divine mission…To help raise the consciousness of humanity and the planet. Let your Twin Flame Love be a purpose for living in joy and fullness. Let it be the love that permeates where everyone you meet becomes full of your love.

From two hearts that beat as one and know it is the love of Twin Flames that holds the universe in its divine embrace; it is the law of the universal magnet—that which is liking unto itself is drawn" (Abraham Hicks). It is said that there is no separating Twin Flames; they will always be eternal! They will always be one ascending on a spiritual path toward their greatness to be.

CHAPTER ONE

JOURNEY OF THE LONELY TALKING AGAIN

There is an unshakable peace you possess that lies deep within yourself. Only you have the power to become your true, authentic crystalline self 'like' your Divine Compliment.

Author:

I returned home from California months prior to me and Curtis crossing paths—not knowing consciously that we were destined to be together. The move to California did not work out and neither did my first marriage. Today, I understand why it was designed that way! I will talk about how my experiences literally became part of my journey toward my greatness to be…

I started over with nothing but my strength and sanity. It was as though I was in the middle of an emotional desert with no refuge in sight, not even a mirage. I found myself having to sleep in a rental car. I would drive looking for employment and visited people with whom I had to spend a night or two with. The times when doors were slammed in my face, I would just drive until I got tired with absolutely nowhere to go! I held firm to the hope for absolution—that was nowhere in sight! My final destination would be the Holiday Inn Hotel parking lot in Runnemede New Jersey, that would soon become my place of temporary residency.

I would sleep some of the time, but was awake most of the time, concerned about my safety and what in the hell was my next move. In the mornings, I would use the hotel restroom to clean myself up to once again look for a job. This would go on for a week. Until one night when I was dead tired and parked earlier than normal, a bright light was shining in the driver side window. It was hotel security! He told me that I could not sleep in the parking lot! Well, there was only one thing to do…Grab hold of my sanity and ask *God Source* to help me go deep down inside to find that radiant spiritual being…*Self.*

My circumstance became despairing after the security warning so I ended up visiting my friend Rosalyn that night. We sat around laughing, talking, and drinking; she could sense that something was wrong. I asked Roz to house me until I could get a place of my own and without hesitation, she said, "Yes! With her support, she allowed me to stay for several months until I got back on my feet. I possessed a great deal of tenacity and persistence. I landed not one but two jobs. I went from a magazine sales rep in the morning to Front Desk Hotel Guest Services in the evening.

Moreover, it was quite convenient in walking distance going from one job to the next. It got to the point where both jobs were weighing on me so I let the magazine job go…

Clap! Clap! Clap! Find A Place
This was one of my Grandmother's old sayings, when we all lived with her on Morton Street in Camden Jew Jersey.

Roz informed me that she and her children would be moving away and that I had 30 days to find a place to live—Clap! Clap! And so…I started looking with the utmost alacrity! I stumbled on a motel room not far from my jobs. I became a regular paying tenant at $620.00 a month. In fact, it was convenient and in walking distance from my job at the hotel. Nevertheless, I did not look forward to the walks at night. Boy was I frightened! While the distance was only about two miles or so, my only concern was walking to and from work. In the midst of me walking to my temporary place of residence, I often wondered what I did wrong and how I ended up in this situation. I thought to myself with a question…" Should I have stayed in the emotional and physical turmoil of a marriage and just dealt with being unhappy?" "Naaaa!" My ex-husband was not renewing the lease to our apartment anyway. I could not go to mom; she told me that I could only stay one night. Much rejection went on! I felt as though I was an outcast…" Black sheep!"

It felt as though a thousand daggers had pierced my heart. I said to myself, "Where does a broken heart go? I mean, really! Is there such a place?" I was missing my daughter Andrea at that time! She was living with my mother! Too embarrassed to tell my daughter that I was living in a hotel and did not want her to see me at my lowest!

I became a very discouraged individual! My mind was confused, my body was tired, my soul seemed lost, and my spirit was broken. It was *just the lonely talking again!* I found *ME*, constantly talking to myself *(those inner voices)*. It was quite an experience having conversations with my inner voices. Whenever someone would pass by me, I would become silent. I did not want people to think that I was "two sandwiches away from a picnic". At that point, in my life, my faith was surely being tested. ***Job, "He knows the way that I take; and when he has tested me, I will come forth as gold." —Job (23:10).***

Stillness Speaks; it is the Language from God!

This experience had me feeling as though I was in a maze, just me all by myself. I was screaming inside and no one was hearing me. The louder I got, the quieter it got on the inside! I mean, you could literally hear a pin drop inside of my head! I knew then that it was time to discover my truest *Self.* **I make the way—I make the path...**

Moreover, here I thought I was in control of the magnanimous illusion that stood before me! I felt that all I have accomplished from that point on vanished like a fart in the wind! Hell, before I knew it, I found myself literally eating humbled pie that put my consciousness in a state of shock. There was a revisit, from an inner voice that I had not heard since I was eleven. You can read about that in my book *"Notes from Women of Timelessness!"* I realized that I possessed one of the most powerful gifts known to man! It was the power of *thought,* and my inner guidance that led me to be still. I did not know that the power of the mind is the second strongest power next to the *Spirit.* I started singing and the universe listened!

Then there was hope!

I no longer needed the approval from that conscious place where contrast abounds...That place where I was engaged in my lonely worries, complaints, and cries! I only yearned for the universe to hear my thoughts, to respond to my vibration and deliver to me all that I desire. This wondrous universe is like a Genie that spoke to me and said, "Your wish is my command." I have been preparing you all along to meet your authentic true self, displaying the *mirror image* of *self...* Your Twin Flame...Your Divine Compliment!

However, in order for this reuniting to take place; I had to become one with **ME**, creating that marriage with mind, body, soul and spirit. I had to make a connection with that radiant spiritual *being—**ME!*** ***Then there was hope!*** An uplifting turn of events had taken place—an unfolding occurred! Something wondrous and divine happened! Together, we were spiritually ready to meet our other *self.* We were ready for our Twin Flameship! There is one thing for certain, and that is, one must first become whole, before two can become ONE! It is said, "That one does not meet his/her Twin Soul or Twin Flame until one has learned many lessons of love, loss, and forgiveness."

CHAPTER TWO

THE 19TH HOLE

Like attracts like...It is the universal magnet...
That, which is liking is drawn.

Curtis' Story

I was sitting at the 19th hole, what we call the clubhouse at Freeway Golf Course in Sicklerville, New Jersey, one year prior to being introduced to my wife. This is how it all began! It happened at one of golf's historically Black Owned Courses, "Freeway" late afternoon on a Wednesday.

During this time, I was Owner-Operator of Riverview Ford Dealership. On Wednesday June 14, 2000, I had just come from Bordentown New Jersey Auto Auction! It was around 2 o'clock pm and I decided to stop at Freeway Golf Course for a quick round of golf with G Lee. After finishing eighteen holes, I decided to have a quick cold one with G Lee at the club house! To my right, there was a door leading to the upstairs of the clubhouse. I was scanning the clubhouse and a beautiful black woman walked through the front door. I said to myself, "Oh my soul!" My attention was pulled in her direction! I noticed her wearing a black and gold cowboy hat. She was looking gorgeous in her blue jeans and wearing one of the biggest belt buckle I had ever seen!

She walked toward me, but in an instant, she walked pass me headed toward a door and just that quick she vanished. Hell, I thought that I owned a big buckle! I had never seen a woman wearing such an enormous silver and gold buckle like that. What stole my heart was the way she carried herself. She possessed a certain presence. She had the utmost assurance and absolute confidence of who she was. I saw a very classy lady!"

I had seen my true Queen in hopes that she would be someone compatible to all that I desired in a woman and would love to do the same things. Honestly she never even noticed me sitting there; she never looked in my direction." I knew nothing about her or who she was! I immediately noticed that there was something unique about her. She was radiant; she was breathtaking to look at if only for that moment…it was as if I had known her all my life. She had opened the door to the Women's locker room and disappeared.

This is where it all began!

She would often say that, "like attracts like!"

One year later, I had absolutely no idea that I would run into her again and that I caught her attention this time. Keep in mind, a year later she noticed me standing outside of the golf course pro shop at Freeway. *Now,* this is the story from Dawn, my wife, (the author of this book) as she tells how our vibrational signals crossed each other's path. At times, she would share with me the few things that we had in common then and now. It really blew my mind when she told me we were Twin Flames and that we share the same soul—it is *ONE*.

She also indicated that a Twin Flame is a complete soul separated during creation only to be reunited. ***She would often say that, "like attracts like!"*** During the time we met, we were both avid golfers taking our worries, frustrations, and concerns to the Tee Box to "lock and load!" To top it off, we were both going through separation and divorce. I can reflect back a couple years ago when she began her quest into Twin Flameship, she indicated how the event that took place on December 21, 2012, played a significant role in our union and why we must stay on the path to ascension.

"Today, I now feel that there is a higher power that brought us together and that we truly are meant to be. Dawn was an amazing beauty with a heart of gold when I met her. Today, my wife is even more beautiful with a bigger heart. She fills me up with her unconditional love and joy…I am truly grateful."

—Curtis J. Bunch

PART II

A SESSION WITH DAWN

You will meet your Twin Flame in unusual circumstances, or at some unexpected place.

The day I met Curtis was the most beloved innocence of a "*love at first sight*" encounter. I was unaware of what it was at that moment, but I knew that God brought me someone that I had been asking for all my life. Today, I share my life, my journey and one soul with my true Twin Flame. Curtis J. Bunch is my Divine Compliment…Love of my life…Life of my love.

And this is my story

There was an intuitive spiritual attraction between Curtis and myself. Neither he nor I had a clue then of what we put out into the universe and that it would come to fruition. It was a vibration of like attracting like. The universe was doing what it does best—responding to vibration. We are vibrational beings in a vibrational universe. We became in alignment to that which we were asking. Truly indeed, it was divine order and the works of this universe that put us in a place of oneness. It was the Law of Allowing that would permeate a vibrational acceptance of reuniting twin flames, sharing one soul, preparing us for our ascension.

Reuniting Twin Flames in apropos and Divine Time

Going back 14 years ago, I can remember it being a hot June day, in the mid-afternoon. It just so happens that on Wednesday June 13, 2001, I was standing in the doorway of Freeway's Golf Course pro shop. I was watching a few of the guys getting ready to head out to play a round of golf. I knew one of guys, Gary Lee! I played several 'Chicken Wing Golf Tournaments with him at Freeway.

In an instant, I heard a male's voice, one that I had never heard since I had been going to Freeway. He had a very loud voice. Well, to satisfy my curiosity, I looked over my left shoulder, identifying where this loud voice was coming from.

When I saw this man, he was making his way up the hill toward the pro shop. I suspected that he was going to join Gary Lee for a round of golf.

Therefore, I waited!

This man stood out on the account of, him not bothering to take the steps; but chose to walk up the hill where the bag drop was. He started talking to Gary Lee, and then he laughed. It was the most earsplitting laugh I had ever heard. In that moment, I did not know what it was that had attracted me to his vibration. Whatever it was, I had to wait around to see! All I knew is that he was not from this 'neck' of the woods. My intuitiveness drew me in! There was a feeling of unwillingness to detach myself from it—I was unable to ignore it…

Today, I would say, God gave me an intuitive nudge that needed my undivided attention. Knock! Knock! Who's there? "Your Intuitive Nudges!" Whenever we ignore them we limit ourselves to the many blessings that God sends us. We pinch ourselves off from who we really are and who we can become.

This time I yielded to a nudge that came from deep inside of me. Back then, I did not know what an intuitive nudge was. Today, I can say that being open to all infinite possibilities that exist through the mind of God, has allowed me to become awakened, enlightened, and fulfilled. ***Therefore, I waited!***

A couple of hours later, this tall man walks into the clubhouse while my friend Wanda and I were sitting at the Lounge. I looked into the mirror, grabbed Wanda by the arm, and said, "There he is! It's him!" All she could say was, "He's tall!" He was getting a few cold ones as they made the turn…He never even looked in my direction!

The sun was going down and Wanda said to me, "How do you know that he is going to come back in?" I said, "Because he is meant to. I just know!" I said to myself, "I don't know where this intense feeling is coming from, but I must stay on the path. At that time, I had no idea the universe responds to all vibrations we put out. I so wanted him to walk through that door again and from what I know today, this universe is like a Genie—little did I know, it would grant me what I desired.

The universe responded and said, "Your wish is my command." Low and behold, this towering man walked into the clubhouse not by himself but with Gary Lee. They sat adjacent to Wanda and I! All I could do was just stare in awe at this strange man that my intuitiveness told me to wait for…My desire the Genie granted me!

There was a powerful divine energy connecting me to this man that was unexplainable and mind you, I did not know him from a can of paint. I chose to be open and receptive to what the universe was giving me. To this day, I believe that he left his energy of the Twin Flame mating call up in Freeway that year he saw me.

Meanwhile, Wanda and I were sitting, drinking our wine and just then, Gary Lee had invited us to sit with them. He said, "Come over here Don"—with his southern accent— "I want you to meet somebody."

With no hesitation, we accepted the invite, got up and walked over to sit down...Gary introduced me to Curtis Bunch. He said, "Curt this is Don, Don this is Curt! Yawl can do the rest! Gary shouted across the bar and said, "What's up lil' bits?" Referring to Wanda, she was only 5'5"! Gary asked, "What yawl doing up in Freeway?" Wanda said, "The same reason why you here...having a beverage... plus, my girlfriend wanted to wait until yawl finished golfing, cause she wanted me to see that tall man, who we never seen at Freeway before. She said something told her to wait and that it was important for her to do just that! She started sounding a little weird, but that's my girl and I got her back!"

This is due to the karmic connection and reflection of one's own soul.

The energy grew stronger! It was as if I had known Curtis all my life. I did not understand what was taking place. All I knew is that I had a feeling come over me, a feeling that I had never felt before. I did not know that we were Twin Flames then, nor that we were a vibrational match—to that which we were asking on a subconscious level. We then exchanged names and he said to me, "Would you believe that I saw you here at Freeway a year ago.

You walked in the front door and went straight up the club house stairs! I waited for you to come back down but you were up there for a while so I left." Then he asked, "Are you a real golfer or a hacker?" I smiled at him and before I could tell it, Gary Lee said, "Oh no Curt, you better watch her, cause this girl can flat out hit a golf ball. She plays from the white tees Curt." Oh, his eyes lit up like silver dollars when he found out that I could 'lock and load' with my Driver and strike a golf ball with my Irons and play competitively. Gary Lee continued, "Hell she'll out drive yo' ass Curt...I bet my money on Don." All Curtis would say was, "I don't believe it!" To this day, Curtis still says that!

I can only guess that a year ago when he saw me, who knew that, I would be in the company of this man golfing together and in a Twin Flame relationship. He had finally crossed paths with a woman who shared one of his passions—playing the game of golf. Little did we know, our lives would never be the same. From that point on, well the rest is history—likened to an unchained melody.

Several weeks had gone by without me seeing him. It was about four o' clock pm. I was working behind the front desk at the Holiday Inn, in Runnemede, NJ. The sliding glass doors open and in walked a man from FTD with what appeared to be three dozen roses. He made his way toward the front desk. I greeted him and asked him, "What guest is receiving this package?" I don't know why my heart was racing! I just knew they were for a guest. But in the back of my mind, I had a feeling that they were for me.

Before the FTD guy could tell me, I was trembling with anxiety! My inner voice gave me an inkling as to who sent them. Deep down inside I knew he was going to ask for me. He said, "Dawn Thomas!"

I put my hands to my mouth totally surprised that my intuition was right on point. There was a small card attached. I opened the card and it read," To a beautiful woman with a beautiful heart—from Curtis." From that point on our union began its journey. That whole day, all I could think about was him sending me his love with three dozen roses. In my head, I started singing Stevie Wonder's song, "Send

One Your Love with a Dozen Roses!" Then I knew that I had to show him my love in return by sending him a dozen of yellow roses to his dealership. We would connect again only to become the manifestation of a divine Rembrandt painted for us by God. Meanwhile, my birthday was approaching and Curtis asked me what my plans were. The only plans I had was to either sit in my hotel room and look at the four walls or go to Freeway and golf! On the day of my birthday, he made plans for us to golf! He arrived in a Ford Harley Davidson pickup truck! He waited until I came out! Curtis was always a gentleman and polite! That showed much about his character. Anyway, when I came out with my clubs ready and dressed for golf, he said, "Close your eyes!" I did, and then he said, "Open them", and I did! I saw a set of golf clubs lying there! He surprised me and said happy birthday. I just smiled, said thank you and embrace him for such a kind gesture. As for my old clubs, I threw them in the garbage!

"My Twin Flame; my Divine Compliment; my True Love."

Ok now I am ready to lock and load with my new clubs! He said, "We have to make a short stop on the way to Wedgewood Country Club. With joy and excitement, "I said ok!" I had no idea where we were headed so I just enjoyed the moment.

We were about twenty minutes into driving and we pulled into a development in Sewell, NJ. We came upon some Condominiums and I am thinking he is just visiting someone. We had pulled up in front of a Condo and he asked me to come with him. So I did!

We got to the door and he gave me a key! Now I don't know what to think! I opened the door and we both walked in. All I saw was an empty living room! We stood in the middle of the floor and he turned to me and said, "Happy Birthday, Dawn". All I could do was cry and said, "You hardly even know me! Why did you do this?"

He said, Remember the flowers that I sent to you on your job and the card said to a beautiful woman with a beautiful heart." "I did it because I saw a loving woman with a beautiful heart, perseverance, and tenacity!" That's rare!" He asked if I liked the place and I said, "It beats living in that hotel paying $600.00 a month, and yes I love it!" I took a glance at my life and saw me go from sleeping in a rental car, to renting a room at a hotel working two jobs to pay for my survival, now I finally have a place that I can call home.

I was truly grateful for his wonderful gesture and the experiences of life's lessons. He said, "Now all we have to do is get YOUR place furnished!" I smiled! All I could do was thank the Creator for allowing our vibrational paths to cross. Today, I realize that it was God's divine plan; to reunite his creation; a soul that was split now joined as one in the physical incarnation.

As I reflect back, us standing inside of that Condo in the middle of an empty living room floor, I saw a Man with a loving heart, and a beautiful spirit filled with light. I saw a man of leadership, integrity, charisma, genuine, and an articulate man with a business mind. I saw a cheerful and devoted friend that happened to be a great golfer. He helped me in my time of need in getting back on my feet. I did not have to ask for anything, because action spoke louder than words. God saw me trying and so did Curtis.

Today, I will always and forever more love and cherish my Twin Flame, my Beloved husband. Today, Curtis and I have acknowledged that we are the rarest of Twin Flames having shared identical mirrored life events. We have taken our rightful place on this planet fulfilling our mission and that is to bring unconditional love, peace, harmony, and mutual respect to all of humanity.

I am the Yielding Twin who holds a heart space for her beloved while fully exploring life on the way to becoming an awakened, illuminated avatar of all human consciousness. Curtis is the Messenger Twin that is allowed the space and freedom to choose to evolve at his own pace in his own way. In other words, this unfolding cannot be forced upon him. You can read more on the stages of Twin Flames later in the book.

Today, I am truly grateful for what God and the Universe has given to me. *"My Twin Flame, my Divine Compliment, my True Love."* And so it is! Ah-shay! Ah-shay! Life is good!"

CHAPTER THREE

TWIN FLAMES

Twin Flameship is a powerful way to anchor light onto the earthly plane!

What is a Twin Flame?

When part of an original soul splits into two parts to form your other *Self,* or *Twin Flame.* A Twin Flame is the mirror image of one soul that has split into two parts, one being male dominant, and the other female. In a sense, a Twin Flames is our other half in another body! hen part of an original soul splits into two parts to form your other *Self,* or *Twin Flame.* A Twin Flame is the mirror image of one soul that has split into two parts, one being male dominant, and the other female. In a sense, a Twin Flames is our other half in another body!

Our soul is made of energy, which is the essence of a blue flame representing what we call a 'Twin Flame.' We now know that during the December 2012 Ascension, more Twin Flames became reunited in mind, body, soul and spirit. During human creation, souls were split to reunite for many lifetimes only to become ONE with your Twin Flame. It is as if a cell was divided, reuniting to the original cell from the very beginning. Twin Flames retain a part of the other within themselves. The yin and yang symbol best illustrates sameness with each side holding a small dot of the other.

Author:

"I know that our Twin Flameship *(my husband and I),* is eternally priceless. It has been divinely paved for us from the very beginning of our existence." Many may not understand the relevance of their connection with the December 2012 Winter Solstice and the significance of a historical time for the planet earth. We did not physically set out on an adventure looking for each other. It was without judgement that we simply became open and receptive to what had already been mapped out for us anyway. Each half became connected through Spirit and vibration. We are one soul that was split, *now joined* (sort of what you would see in the Bible), which has some validity to *(two becoming one)!* Twin Flames are two becoming one *"again!"* We all have a desire to seek true love because we long for the connection to Mr. or Ms. Right. Remember, in order for this union to take place you must possess those same wholesome, loving, happy, healthy, joyous and peaceful characteristics as your Twin Flame.

In the Bible, we see marriage as "A man shall leave his father and mother and cling to his wife and they shall become one flesh" and, "What God has joined together let no man part." *(Matthew 19: 5, 6).* The Twin Flame union is the only one in which this is truth instead of just representational by a contract of marriage. Twin Flames are eternally married in their very being, something that no one can change.

Twin Flame and Soul Mates Are Not the Same

Please, let us not confuse Twin Flame and Soul Mates! They are not the same. People have a misconception that their Soul Mate is actually Your Soul Mate may possess Twin Flame qualities, but they are not your true one and only Twin Flame.

Your Twin Flame is the spiritual connection to you on a Soul Level from the beginning of time. This is a very special spiritual union at a higher 'Self' and Soul Level.

Often times we subconsciously yearn for our Twin Flame but to no avail, we just cannot find that perfect partner. You may be in a union right now and still your standards and expectations are high. In this case they are not met. We are often disappointed. Therefore, whether you are with your Twin Flame or Soul Mate, you cannot expect that person to make you whole it is not their job! They will disappoint you every time. Your wholeness comes to you through a connection with your *Spiritual Self.* You must establish a union with your *Spiritual Self.* You must be tuned it, tapped in, turned on and connected to those vibrational frequencies.

Are you ready to meet the authentic YOU?

Those are the indicators of unconditional love, lovingness, and love intellect that you are graced with. You can certainly ask God to bring you your Twin Flame through your current spouse or significant other.

Whoever your partner is in this life, whether it is your Soul Mate, Twin Soul, or Twin Flame, no union will ever be absolutely perfect, due to the physical incarnation; our human side with many lessons and karma. But you can make your union *perfect* there is a such thing…The Twin Flame Souls are mastered in divine love. We are all trying to find this original divine love of our soul whether we are aware of it or not! The eagerness is there and will always be! Together, you must become infused with the all loving; all knowing divine love, that which makes it *perfect*.

Vibration Is Everything

All of creation is made up of vibrating energy that never dies…it is a force that is at a continuum. It is constant and unwavering! Twin Flames can be explained as two individuals vibrating exactly on the same frequency, sharing identical characteristics within their being. Your Twin Flame is the only one that will match this exact pattern of hormonal identity.

When in the presence of your Twin, you can feel the increase of vibrational 'love energy' the very being of your souls is in constant connection. The vibes you share feel so comfortable, a feeling that is so very natural, but yet so intense. The Twin Flame is seen almost instantly on soul level and the physical appearance is somewhat identical. The similar characteristics that exist among Twin Flames are extraordinary. Their strength on the inside, which sparks that flame within their hearts. Sometimes their conscious mind is unable to figure out what the attraction is right away.

This can be a deterrent and cause a person to want to back away from this unfolding or deny it until they have figured it out which in some cases; never. Such energy can be quite forceful, that it may even defy all that one desires in connecting to their Twin Flame. At times, we may have felt energy for Soul Mates with whom we had life experiences with but the Twin Flame encounter is always the most intense energy as well as the most life-changing emergence. It is an unfolding upward toward true Twin Flameship. There is only one beautiful, perfect complement to each person's soul…his or her Twin Flame. *Are you ready to meet the authentic YOU?*

What is Twin Flameship?

It is within the circle of cosmic universal love, *self,* and your Twin Flame. This union is the destiny of Twin Flames ascending together. It is quite rare of Twin Flames to incarnate at the same time. Thus having shared mirrored life experiences like myself and my husband Curtis. When Twins are united there may be extraordinary circumstances such as an age difference or that one or both of them are already married or in a committed union. When Twin Flames get to know each other they will feel as if the other is reading their life script. That is not to say they are identical people, but they are perfectly complimentary to each other. When Twin Flames meet for the first time in a physical life, they recognize themselves in the other person. This will come as a deep surprise to both, but the attraction is immediate.

Why Twin Flame Reunion May Take So Long

Many of you have been wondering, and for quite some time, "Where is your Twin Flame and why doesn't he/she seem to respond to my vibration?" There is a very simple reason…It is because of **YOU!** It is evident that you are just not ready to meet the other YOU! Your other authentic *self!* As stated earlier, everyone was created with a Twin Flame, a Divine Compliment! So yes, you are bucking your own current because of fear from all the karmic energy that you carry until you deal with it and release it. Whether it is rejection, disappointment, or hurt from the past experiences in your life this hinders you from moving pass that old stuff, and ultimately, halting your desired future. When there is discord and uncertainty going on in your life's script, you are the deliberate creator of that reality. If you desire to become connected with your Twin Flame you must get out of your own way.

Your Twin has been mostly out of his/her third Dimensional Self, just to be in their/your fully incarnated Higher Self Presence, in order to help you, guide you, and prepare both of you for physical Twin Flame Reunion.

After the December 21, 2012 Ascension, what is occurring now is an unfolding for many, as their own Higher Self/ Soul Presence will now be entering and fully emerging into their fourth Dimensional Physical body. Now we are fully prepared and capable of holding our True High Divine Love and its expansive high vibration in a fifth Dimensional Consciousness! The Twin Flame experience is only for those whom are truly ready to embrace their authentic crystalline *self.* There are those who are prepared to really roll up their sleeves and get downright dirty with the *Stuff* of misaligned egos while digging for the ultimate treasure of finding his or her true *self!*

This union can also be an ultimate challenge here on Earth; removing all karma can a bit overwhelming. It is not at all glitter and gold, but both can overcome the adversities that he or she is faced with by simply yielding to this divine plan that was put in place for the Twin Flames.

CHAPTER FOUR

THEY DO IT WITH MIRRORS

Twin Flame unions are very unique unions
within itself that gives the world love.

Dealing with Your Mirrors

The certain past life events of Twin Flames have mirrored each other almost exactly. They may have come from very similar families and family dynamics. They may have had similar schooling. They may have crossed paths socially or may have lived close to each other but have never known it. They may even have had previous marriages and divorces within weeks of each other.

At the same time, Twin Flames will feel that they have always known that person who is sitting in front of them. It is a feeling of homecoming, because you recognize your other self and feel very much that you have come home when you are with your spiritual Twin Flame...your *ultimate* Soul Mate.

Twins Flames often can sense what the other is doing and feeling!

Upon meeting one's Twin, it is said that there is an immediate connection and attraction toward each other. This is like a love at first sight vibration. Twin Flames will often meet in the most un-canning moments at an unexpected time. The energy felt between Twin Flames is much like an explosion! The relationship among them is like no other! Their connection is as stated earlier—through the soul!

The union between Twin Flames must come from a spiritual, soul-centered stance not from human insecurities, controlling habits or patterns of a physical realm.

Twin Flames often resemble each other in appearance. It is common for them to appear related as well as complement one other physically and characteristically. Twin Flames share the same natural rhythm and vibrations. They have a natural energy and vibration that can be felt by anyone who is in close proximity to them.

Twins Flames often can sense what the other is doing and feeling! Twin Flames share the same vibrations—they share a connection that is often telepathic. One Twin is usually very connected to spirit. It is common for Twins to share similar thoughts and feelings simultaneously, feeling each other's emotions and energy when they are not in each other's presence. Twin Flames often can sense what the other is doing and feeling! At times, their communication can be somewhat on a telepathic vibration when they are apart! Everything about the Twin Flame connection is strong spiritually, and perhaps even magical in a sense.

There are 12 Dimensions but 11:11 is a powerful phenomenon that exists within the 12 dimensions of the universe. The numbers the 11:11 are the highest spiritual number in the 11th Dimension. Within the 11th dimension, Twin Flames are the numbers 11:11 (eleven eleven)…Twins are surrounded with the profound significance of such mystical numbers. Dates, ages, and anything pertaining to the Twins and numbers will often become 11 11. For those who are in awareness with Twin Flames, one could meet them and they instantly see 11:11. Twin Flames are profound and unlike any other. The significance of such a divine natural feeling can escape the conscious mind as thinking nothing more than, it was meant to be that way.

Now in the 12th dimension of consciousness Twin Flames are alongside the God head. They see things from the total point of view of oneness and see everything as if they were looking down from the highest place. Once a person realizes their connection to their Twin Flame on the inside they will be able to experience this dimension of consciousness. This supersedes all polarity and all separation! It might take a while to realize just how unique and perfect that one person was meant for you and why—but on the soul level, it knows it instantly.

The reason 11:11 is for Twin Flames is this…they are able to subconsciously lift themselves into that dimension of higher consciousness—the all-knowing mind…accepting the realization that Twin Flames are created as one soul split into male and female.

However, there are other mirrored numbers that are also common to see like 12:12 11:22 12:21. Once you begin to understand why these numbers play a significant role in all human existence, you will subconsciously be in the presence of your mirror image, your truest love…in the physical realm! Keep in mind of the healing process of self! It will almost undoubtedly have to happen for all of us on many lower dimensional levels before we can be united permanently with our Twin Flame, it is still known and seen as we operate on all these levels.

So is a sense, 11:11 is a state of consciousness that is really all about noticing your mirror image from one dimension to the next—it is eternal. Your Twin Flame is the exact mirror of you inside the same way the number mirrors itself. You may begin to see mirroring things in your life—well within this dimension too. Take a look at the 11:11 illustration on page 36 and the Pyramid illustration on page 37.

Author

"Curtis and I share the number 11:11 in our birth dates, age, last names, second number of our S.S.# and our daughter's birth date.

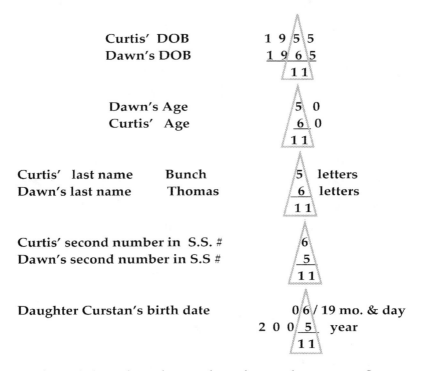

Curtis' DOB	1 9 5 5	
Dawn's DOB	1 9 6 5	
	1 1	
Dawn's Age	5 0	
Curtis' Age	6 0	
	1 1	
Curtis' last name	Bunch	5 letters
Dawn's last name	Thomas	6 letters
		1 1
Curtis' second number in S.S. #	6	
Dawn's second number in S.S #	5	
	1 1	
Daughter Curstan's birth date	0 6 / 19 mo. & day	
	2 0 0 5 year	
	1 1	

Eleven (11) is where that single soul was split into two flames at the very basic level of pure energy that which is anchored to the third dimension. However, we do share 10:10 in which both of our first names have a total of 10 letters and that we are 10 years' apart age wise. Thus entering into the 10th dimension of consciousness. We are always consciously in alignment on the soul level of such consciousness. The Twin Flame soul mate is able to feel things the other is going through, feel their emotions and sometimes know their thoughts because they share the same larger soul.

They can feel them inside their own chest just as the dot resides in the yin yang. Here is a more detailed chart of our divine connection.

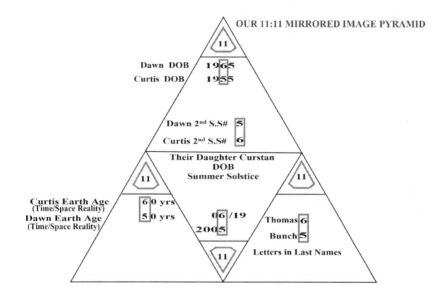

OUR 11:11 MIRRORED IMAGE PYRAMID

The make-up of the Twin Flames is such that, one is male with a tiny piece of the female inside it and one female with a tiny piece of the male inside—it shares the same values and significance of yin yang. Twin Flames love to be together through the connectedness, and that lovemaking is the ultimate expression of this unity of *ONENESS*. The bond between Twin Flames can be so passionate during lovemaking that the connection alone is as good as having a pure orgasm. Twin Flames can be apart and yet feel that level of extreme sexual vibration to that of a 'mating' call—only with their Twin Flame are they receptive, especially under the Lunar moons, which amplifies that energy.

It is common for Twin Flames to share similar thoughts and feelings simultaneously; feeling each other's emotions and energy even when they are not in each other's presence. They share the same natural rhythm and vibrations as well as a connecting awareness of what the other is doing and feeling. This connection is often intuitive among each other. While one Twin Flame is connected to spirit, the other Twin becomes open and receptive and everything about their connection is ever so wonderful. Hey, it is not the end of the world if you are not with your Twin Flame right now.

Everything happens for a reason, as it may be learning experiences in that moment as well as blessings in each of your life's journey toward your Twin Flameship. Now if you have gotten this far in the book, you should be eager—not just eager—but willing to read on further. *"Mirror Image"* has shared with you the dynamics of Twin Flames and Twin Flameship. By now, you may be at a crossroad on whether to close this book and tell yourself, by some deep-rooted thought that this is all bulls$@t! On the other hand, you are curious enough to find out if perhaps you are with your Twin Flame, will meet your Twin Flame and by some divine force that your Twin Flame will appear in an instant. You know—like on your doorstep! I got news for you! Your Twin Flame is always present, and will surface when *you* are ready to meet them. So, what are you waiting for? Your Twin Flame subconsciously is knocking at your door right now! You are just not letting them in! "Why you asked?" Here are three reasons:

- Fear of meeting your true authentic *Self.*
- Not being true to *SELF*
- Caught up in the illusion of *Self-Definition*

Hell, you didn't know right! The words in this book will not determine your course of action your own thoughts will.

This book is based on a "true love story, a Twin Flame reuniting, our mirrored life experiences to now and not bulls$@t, it does value your opinions though. Moreover, we all know what opinions are "Like a$$-holes, everybody's got one!" At its best, our story may be one of the most inspiring truths on the perfect union by far. The passion of two sharing at the innermost levels of all that is, our bodies, our lives, our breath, our thoughts and our hearts, becoming open and receptive completely to merge our spirits for the transmutation of love. This is the divine marriage and nothing can destroy this union, because we have detached ourselves from all illusions.

This Divine chemistry creates an all-powerful whirlwind through which Divine Love can flow, anchoring our light onto this Earthly plane. When the Twin Flame union reaches this stage it begins the ascension of the work well under way. Both having detached all their previous karmic connections through their mirrored life experiences and becoming drama free. Now they become sovereign *beings* possessing the Christ like consciousness together…joined as one. One soul inhabits the essence of two physical avatars manifested here on Earth with the divine plan of really making a difference. Curtis and I have been reunited, helping to create union based love portals to help build and restore unbalance and disharmony in personal relationships with God, *self*, and others. We service all of humanity, we love unconditionally and a life of happiness and well-being in abundance. Twin Flame unions are unique within itself giving love to the world love. They possess extraordinary yet almost identical thought pattern, like Twins born from the same birth sac. It is amplified with the tendency to mirror what they do physically without having to be in each other's company. It is no wonder that these two lovers are as *one*…constantly in alignment of the same shared passions. They offer unwavering unconditional love as Twin Flame lovers often do.

To those who is seeking Twin Flameship, your common goal here is to continue on the path of ultimate personal growth and freedom. You become centered, you bring balance, and make that connection with your true inner self. Your Twin Flame will answer…

...They will come! Keep in mind that it is possible to ask God to manifest your Twin Flame through your present lover, or to guide you to your Twin. Before this can happen, you must recognize the presence of your true authentic crystalline self, and then you must recognize the presence of your Twin Flame.

Everyone has a Twin Flame and you are destined to be together. Love makes the world go around, and as this world turns, Twin Flame love is everywhere. This intense eternal connection and power of the flames gives new meaning to the Gospel of Matthew 19:6 which is traditional and quoted in wedding ceremonies." It is because of what God has joined together that makes Twin Flames their divine compliment—their "Mirror Image"!

Read what others have to say!

Rev. Shaneetha Akinlana the Love Doctor
Twin Flames ~ The Ultimate Relationship

We have many soul mates in life but only one twin flame. **There is only one that was created with you when time began. There is only one with the same blueprint, one with the same identity patterns, and with the same spark of life as you.** Your twin flame is the highest path of initiation on the physical plane that you will experience. It is the pure love of all humanity. It is the marriage to the soul to god; God is perfect love.

We are all co- creators with God, just a little lower than the angels. In the beginning, when God was shaking, rattling, and rolling, when all that creating was going on in the universe, there was one big sacred pause in the universe of time and space. God said let there be light and there was. (Genesis 1:3). You were a flame and a part of that divine light. We all know the story of how God divided everything into two: night and day, sun and moon, male and female, birth and death, young, old, and the list go on.

At that time in creation, twin flames were also divided into two halves, masculine and feminine. Each, an aspect of the same singular energy sent to one part of the universe for its individual necessary expression, and the other individual spirit energy sent to another part of the universe for it's necessary individual expression. This parallel of the nature of twin flame duality has always been a part of existence.

Every human being possesses a twin flame.

Although you were separate at the beginning of time to have your necessary individual experiences on the physical plane or other man-ifestation, you never lost contact with each other. The contact is con-tinuous. The flowing in and out of energy and information is happing even now, as you read these words. It can never be interrupted. It can never be tampered with. The communication and contact continues unabated on inner levels. The bond can never be broken. This is where you are held encased together in the mind of God. The casual body is protected with the illuminating light of purity between God and man. The energy of twin flames. It is on higher levels, it is the balancing of alpha and omega energies. the father and mother, the yin and yang, and the spiral eight figures. If you look closely at the point in the middle of the figure eight where the connecting circle meet, and the energy begins to move upward and downward, this is where the casual body lies and cannot be altered, adulterated, or touched by man's thoughts, words or deeds. The casual body is encapsulated in the mind of God, like the peanut inside of the M&M candy; you cannot see the peanut but you know it is there.

The law of creation is one of division and reunion. Somewhere in the memory of each twin flame soul there is longing to be reunited. At a point, they will become androgynous once again. It is said that we all must incarnate on the physical plane with seven masculine embodiments and seven feminine embodiments, with each lasting about seven thousand years. After a period of 14,000 years (give or take a few thousand years), we can be reunited. After much evolving, we are given the opportunity to balance 100% of our karma in order to take our ascension to higher octaves.

Because of God's grace and mercy during this special dispensation of the 21st century, we now only have a balance 51% of our karma. In addition, to the seriousness of our planet, we were also given the special dispensation of the violet flame. The violet flame is also known as the mercy flame. Twin flames are also given this special dispensation to come together again in large numbers at this time in history. Their work together is to help save the planet. The new millennium holds great blessing and great challenges for those who seek truth. Relationships and marriages are falling apart at an alarming rate and short-term marriage contacts provide us with long- term pain. Children are inevitably left in the gap with drugs, lack of training, little respect for elders, and nasty music to distort their fertile minds.

Commitment means, *until I am ready to stop loving you,* which comes way too soon. We lack honesty of thought in marriage and relation-ship. Sex is at an all-time high. Trust and respect is at an all-time low. Men and women lack understanding of their roles in relationships. Husbands, wives, and significant others do not seek times in common prayer, meditation, and ritual together. We are religious but lack true spirituality.

Whether you are in a positive or negative relationship, all of your ex-periences go back to your twin flame. Every experience you will ever have is preparing you for your twin flame. On your road home to be recognized with your beloved, there is bound to be pain and suffering as the little ego dies.

Nevertheless, these are necessary paths to fulfillment and higher consciousness. We must remember to continue to love in the face of challenge and adversity. We must begin to recognize our relationships are a part of the spiritual path, the path that leads us back to our true nature or God-self.

We must begin to call to our twin flames and use the violet flame to help release fear blockages in the seven chakras. We must let go of resentment in ourselves and all other parts of life. Remember, there are no failures on the spiritual path, only karmic lessons and life expe-rience learned. The greatest amount of light that is being released on the physical plane at this time in history is that which is most greatly being opposed. That is our love for one another. Always remember, the greatest act of love and kindness is humility. Be humble to all and you will succeed your greatest wishes and desires. Relationships are necessary to our spiritual growth. Love gives us a chance to balance our heart, body, and soul. The true opportunity is to learn to love ourselves. I believe every action is meant to move us all forward with love and union with our twin flame. It is a fact that man and woman come together to reveal one another *to* each other.

Loving relationships occur when we learn to love ourselves and the other person unconditionally. Our greatest cosmic reward on earth and in heaven is to receive our twin flames. We must call to our twin flame and use the violet flame to release the fear blockages and forgivingness of self. Have faith as all prayers are answered in time and space.

Twin Flames Productions http://www.twinflamesinlove.com

CHAPTER FIVE

FINDING BALANCE

Each half must find balance in their male/female,
yin yang before this union can manifest.

Don't Fear Your Twin Flame; it's The Other You

There is an intensity that may frighten you when dealing with your "mirror or your other self!" Your weaknesses and strengths become magnified, unresolved issues and painful wounds open, causing your mind to think *abandon ship* or *haul ass* from your Twin Flame relationship. There is much work to be done when creating a balance as you prepare for this unfolding.

You have to be totally immersed in life, not yielding to the resistance of it but appreciating the radical amazement of life, the pleasure, the pain, the joy, and the tears. It is not about denying your human experiences. It is divine poetry in motion that plays out the Twin Flameship…emerging from the pages of life. When both halves of the Soul become dedicated in their journey to reunite with their Twin, they have healed and resolved any karmic ties in the present life, and they can now unite to fulfill their Divine purpose. However, the adversities do not end.

Being in Balance with Mind, Body, Soul, and Spirit

This plan of action calls for much prayer, meditation, Chakra Cleansing, and Healing because there is no other way around this sacred connection with *self.* You must come to know who *you* are in mind, body, soul, and spirit.

When you are balanced then you become open and receptive to the all the is-ness well within the realm of Twin Flameship. Things will become quite evident and you will begin to make sense of it all. Many spend their entire life trying to make sense of it all trying to put pieces in where they do not fit but try and force them anyway. When you are not balanced, it may seem that nothing around you is balanced. Now do you understand the importance of why balance is well needed in your life?

This is where the illusion comes into play...The trickery sets the Ego's wheels in motion. Just imagine meeting up with your Twin Flame and you are nowhere near balanced! It will be like looking into the mirror and you saying to yourself, "I am so not ready for *me*!" On a subconscious level is essentially what your other half would feel— within their own thoughts! Neither ready nor willing to be with *you* because *you* are not receptive and your vibrational frequencies are off. As a result, your other half no longer desires to play with you in the sand box! In other words, you fore meeting your Twin or against it. You just simply have to get it right! You must

The one gift that you can give yourself, is to become balanced!

possess those same characteristics that you would want in a person that you feel you want to spend the rest of your life with.

The key is to get rid of the karmic drama that you have acquired over the course of thousands of years that you have been evolving. Know that your Twin Flame has done, is doing, and will do the same. Keep in mind, there is one of you that may be more spiritually in-tune than the other. Together you must be in harmony with *self* and become balanced with the mind, body, soul, and spirit.

Becoming balanced with *self* is the greater, most significant part of this process. It is through a spiritual awakening portal consisting of prayer, meditation, chakra cleansing and healing, and the ultimate unfolding of *self-anew*. **The one gift that you can give yourself, is to become balanced!**

Prayer

Dawn and Curtis' Twin Flame Prayer

We acknowledge through our ascension and we accelerate our progression on our spiritual path toward our greatness to be. We look to God our Higher Self (the I AM Presence) and our Holy Spirit to create a spiritual connection with that inner light of divinity.

We acknowledge that we share one soul and that we are a spark of God. We acknowledge that it is our mission to help raise the consciousness of humanity and the planet through our collective energy; acting upon the hidden energy, that love is the only answer that binds us all into a collective good.

We invoke the presence of God through our unconditional love and mutual respect to all humanity and the planet. When we hold each other in the Highest Light, we look to our Holy Spirit for guidance and wisdom. We release all negative karma and self-limiting beliefs. We yield to the full expression of our divine self and the spiritual enlightenment of our divine mission.

We may be worlds apart but will always unite our Twin Flame spiritually and on higher planes. This spiritual connection intensifies that inner light of divinity that we each possess. The power of our unconditional love enables us to stand strong through life's challenges. Our divine love fortifies and fulfills our Spirit bringing balance to any karmic connections.

We look to our Third Eye Chakra that corresponds with our intuition, consciousness, and intuitive ability, to channel psychic through our spiritual energy. Thus giving us the power to release any negative thought patterns that try to keep us from staying connected with our higher self. We acknowledge that our Twin Flameship remains unwavering to our divine flame of oneness.

Twin Flame Victory Prayer

"In the name of my Higher Self and the Higher self of my beloved Twin Flame. I call to the blessed I Am Presence of our twin flames for the sealing of our hearts as one, for the victory of our divine purpose.

I invoke the light of the Holy Spirit, and the Ascended Masters, Angels, Hosts of Light, and (include your personal angels, guides, councils, etc.) Who will sponsor uniting my Twin Flame and I in the physical. I call for the consuming of all portents of our returning negative karma, clouding our ability to recognize each other and creating a sense of separation.

I call to dissolve the human imposed self-limitations that keep us from the full expression of our Twin Flame identity and the fulfillment of our original contract with Spirit in service to mankind."

If you say this prayer often and aloud, you are stating to the universe your intention to be united with your Twin Flame. The incredible strength of Twin Flame love will empower you to stand strong against the challenges and initiations that inevitably come to all those who desire to be love. All other relationships are secondary to the Twin Flame.

Even if your Twin Flame is not in embodiment at this time, or available for relationship on the level you seek, rest assured you are united spiritually, and never separated through your Higher Self. No man can separate what Source has joined together. Utilizing the power of prayer and pure intention, the light you invoke will clean up the mutual negative karma between you and your Twin Flame.

The Age of Aquarius is the age of Twin Flames and soul mates coming together in love to anchor in our Golden Age. We are the forerunners of this Great Golden Age dawning. The power of love between Twin Flames and soul mates spreads out into our communities and their love heals us all.

Written by Author Kelley Rosano
DBA: Kelley Rosano, LLC
620 S. Vance St. Suite 1146
Lakewood, Colorado 80226

Source Referenced: http://www.kelleyrosano.com/

The Relevance of Twin Flames and You

There may be some confusion as to how it is that only one pair of a Twin 'set' may be incarnated here on earth. That is due to the nature of the Twin Flame energy, although it is not necessary for both Twins to be present. Only one Twin's physical incarnation may be present in order for this vortex of energy to be felt by both Twins.

What matters is that each Twin no matter where they are will be able to live and exist within that Twin Flame vibration. When both are doing this, the energy becomes a physical manifestation on earth. However, when both Twins feel off, they are merely resisting to the likeness of whatever feelings, emotions or expressions they are not willing to deal with at that moment. This is where the concept of the Twin Flame Energy Meditation comes into play. The reunion of Twin Flame's sole purpose is their commitment to working together to bring about spiritual evolution toward humanity.

Chakra Cleansing and Healing

"Beloved, I pray that you may prosper in all things and be in health, just as your soul prospers." Three John 1:2 (NKJV)

Every chakra point in your body represents the universal color spectrum called R.O.Y.G.B.I.V. The color spectrum is something that you learned in your high school physics class. Now in Yogic and Buddhist traditions it is believed that the body is made up of both the physical and astral bodies, both of which function separately but have the ability to affect the state of the other. These traditions believe that, like the nervous system, the astral body also has an energy system made up of seven major chakra points that allows energy to enter and leave the body.

Now whether you believe it or not your chakras have everything to do with you the total *you* and your entire DNA make-up. We are made of energy and knowing that you have control of this energy at all times is quite enlightening! You always have the power to control your thoughts and energy by paying attention to the way you feel both internal and external. You do not have to agree with what you are reading in this book. Even the Bible speaks about the body temple and good health…" To prosper in health as your soul prospers!"

Now with regard to the seven-chakra points, they are located in the core of your body, from your tailbone to the crown of your head. When your chakras are closed, your mind, body, soul, and spirit are not in harmony. The author of this book is living proof that Chakra Cleansing and Healing will bring happiness, harmony and balance into your life. It is beyond the fountain of youth. When you make this cleansing and healing applicable to your daily life, you will find yourself living life according to the Gospel of John.

Opening Up to the Healing Energy of Our Divine Light through Chakra Points in the Body

Your Chakras are the seven power points of life force in the body.

Root Chakra: RED
VITALITY, COURAGE, SELF CONFIDENCE

This is the first chakra and its energy center is located down the base of your spine and groin area. This is the animal or base nature. You will see or feel a glowing beautiful shade of red light, spinning like a fan.

This chakra heals your finances, your career, your home life, and all of your possessions. Everything that you desire comes to you easily on the wings of the angles! Your root chakra will become illumined and even brighter red throughout the base of your spine when you release old fears about money. When you detach old self-limiting beliefs, you move into the new energy paradigm, where your desires are a manifestation through joyful work. When you exchange what you love to do you get all the support you need in this material world. Balancing this chakra gives energy to the physical body, controls fear, increases overall health, and helps to be grounded. Give thanks right now and know that it is so! You are perfect, whole, and complete.

Healing Stones for the root chakra are the Hematite, garnet, black obsidian, smoky quartz, red jasper, jet, bloodstone, ruby, and fire opal. Its planets are Earth and Saturn.

Sacral Chakra: ORANGE
HAPPINESS, CONFIDENCE, RESOURCEFULNESS

This is the second chakra and its energy center is located at the genitals. It is below your stomach. You will see or feel a glowing beautiful shade of orange light, spinning like a fan.

This chakra monitors sexuality, reproduction, and procreation. The center of creativity and appetite that connects you from the spirit world to the material world. Balancing this chakra brings vitality, physical power, and fertility. When cleansed, the orange glowing light becomes brighter and vivid. Through your expanded consciousness, you possess the ability to bring joy to your workday and strengthen your appetite for life. Healing Stones for the sacral chakra is the

Carnelian, orange calcite, orange jasper, fire opal, and tiger's eye. Its celestial body is the Moon.

Solar Plexus Chakra: YELLOW
WISDOM, CLARITY, SELF-ESTEEM

This is the third chakra and its energy center is located above the naval. This magical energy center is like the sunshine. You will see or feel a beautiful shade of yellow light, spinning like a fan. It Gives us clarity of thought, increases our awareness, and stimulates interest and curiosity. The energy from this chakra connects us to our mental self. This chakra relates to our self-worth on how we feel about ourselves and how others perceive us. Balancing this chakra calms your emotions and frustration, easing any tension that stand in the way of your intuitiveness. You feel much more in control of your life. You are in control that your free will choices mirror God's Will. All of your defenses are relaxed. You are allowing yourself to *be*.

Healing Stones for the Solar Plexus Chakra are the citrine, yellow jasper, amber, fire opal, golden calcite, topaz, and moonstone. Its planets are Mars, and the Sun.

Heart Chakra: GREEN
BALANCE, LOVE, SELF CONTROL

This is the fourth chakra and its energy center is located in the center of the chest. You will see or feel a big, glowing ball of emerald green light spinning like a fan. This chakra is of love/self-love. It has the ability to give and take unconditionally. Green connects us to unconditional love and is used for balancing our whole being. This light is eradicating and healing any emotional pain that we may have suffered in any lifetime including this one. Your heart is the connection between you and God. It is love; its inner state is compassion and love. Its energy brings powerful healing, and all the information that you need to guide you safely and harmoniously every moment. Balancing this chakra's energy center, you are an automatic powerful healer for the circulatory system, heart, and thymus. It helps relax muscles, nerves, and thoughts. We are able to give unconditional love and also to love and nurture ourselves. There is a feeling of renewal, peace, and harmony. Every good thing comes to you in this world with an open heart. You attract beautiful opportunities to become a part of loving peaceful relationships. The Angels guard and protect your heart by giving you intuitive nudges that you must adhere to and listen to when you come across someone in the physical or non-physical world with lower energy. If you trust the Angels messages that come through your intuition, it is safe for you to love and to be loved by the same vibrational frequency of pure unconditional love. Trust your intuition and know that you are loved.

Healing Stones for the Heart Chakra are the rose quartz, pink tourmaline, green aventurine, rhodochrosite malachite, jade, peridot, and rhodonite. Its planet is Venus.

Throat Chakra: BLUE
KNOWLEDGE, HEALTH, DECISIVENESS

This is the fifth chakra and its energy center is located in the Throat. You will see or feel a beautiful shade of blue light circle, spinning like a ceiling fan. It is the color of the spirit and is connected to self-expression, speech, communication, and creativity. It gives us the ability to communicate our needs and desires, Spirit of truth and purpose. It connects us to holistic thought, and gives us wisdom and clarity, enhancing communication and speech. Balancing this chakra allows your higher self and Holy Spirit to speak through you in all of your communications. You must step back and let Spirit lead the way.

All of your communications are perfectly ordered and guided. Everyone with whom you come into contact will benefit through your communications as it will permeate through them.

Healing Stones for the Throat Chakra are Turquoise, sodalite, blue calcite, aquamarine, blue lace agate, and blue aragonite. Its planets are Mercury and Neptune.

Brow Chakra (Third Eye): INDIGO
INTUITION, MYSTICISM, UNDERSTANDING

This is the sixth chakra and its energy center is located in the center of the forehead above the eyebrows. The color opens the consciousness, brings awareness to higher planes, and connects us with the spiritual world. It connects us to our new, spiritual vision, our unconscious self, and gives us the experience of being part of the whole universe. When you are willing to release all fear of seeing the future, of seeing the truth, you will discover the hidden meanings within this chakra. Awareness is found in the deep purple folds of our innermost selves.

The indigo energy strengthens intuition, imagination, psychic powers, and increases dream activity. It is like returning to our root chakra emanating up through ourselves through the chakra spine only to meet our true, authentic selves with new understanding. Balancing this chakra helps psychic perception and balances the pineal gland. As you anchor your new spiritual vision, you are safe. Affirm that your vision is perfectly ordered and illuminated by love.

Healing Stones for the Brow Chakra are the Lapis lazuli, sugilite, azurite, celestite, blue aventurine, and angelite. Its planet is Jupiter.

Crown Chakra: VIOLATE/PURPLE
BEAUTY, CREATIVITY, INSPIRATION

This is the seventh chakra and its energy center is located inside the top of the head. See or feel this majestic purple circle twirling around like a ceiling fan getting brighter and brighter. The energy connected with your higher self and the universal all-knowing mind. This chakra takes you deep into your awareness perspective. As you become illumined and awakened through your cosmic awareness, its inner state is bliss. This is the color of cosmic awareness and cosmic consciousness. It is a unifying color of oneness and spirituality, self-knowledge and spiritual awareness. It is the union with your higher self, with spirituality, and your higher consciousness. Should there be an in-balance of energy in this chakra? It is because of either too much or too little! This can result in your body to at a *Dis-ease*.

We must allow the violet energy to connect us to our spiritual self-bringing, guidance, wisdom, and inner strength and purify our thoughts and feelings, that which gives us inspiration in all of our affairs. Balancing this chakra, you allow the light of your Holy Spirit to dissolve all barriers to divine wisdom and guidance.

Affirm that you are perfectly safe as you follow your spiritual inner guidance. I am a power loving spiritual *being*. The energy of this color enhances artistic talent and creativity. It allows me to listen, trust, and take guided action.

Healing Stones for the Crown Chakra are Amethyst, white topaz, white calcite, blue opal and blue sapphire. Its planet is Uranus.

When you cleanse and heal your chakras, you will become fully illumined. Your Spiritual wisdom will become fully awakened and activated. Take this moment and give thanks to God, your Angles, and your Holy Spirit for your awakened Spiritual power.

Affirmation: I am fully immersed in the warm, glowing beauty of my true self. I am perfect, whole, and complete. I am very, very LOVED.

"It is our Divine Connectedness through the Heart Chakra that allows the expansion of our mind, body, soul, and spirit anew—to flow freely through the ascending love portal of this Twin Flame Union. Because you are beautiful, I love you; heaven knows I do. Whatever our future together—we were meant to be... After all, this Is how we were created."

"We became the illumination...from the Highest Light."

—Dawn M. Bunch

The Balancing Act with Chakra Cleansing, Healing and Meditation

I am in alignment to that which I am asking from Source. I remain Eternally Blissful, Whole, and Complete. I am reborn and awakened to the many truths of the I AM Presence, validating my Ascension...accepting realization that I am a Spark of God. For I am INFINITE, I am SPIRIT, I am ONE with God!

CHAPTER SIX

TWIN FLAME ASCENSION

*We stand at the dawn of a miraculous
new evolution for humanity.*

What is Ascension?

Whether we know it or believe it, we are constantly unfolding into a higher vibrational reality that consists of unconditional love, joy, and mutual respect for all life. In this new dimension, the reality exists here and now. It is all around us…present everywhere in its fullness. What does this mean? How will it affect you? The answer is that it already has but you are just not aware of it. Put it this way; the affect is truly Heaven on Earth…beyond your wildest expectations.

December 21, 2012 was the time of ascension. This was the ultimate connection of the author and her husband—it was their validation as Twin Flames in the physical embodiment. Many Twin Flame couples have come together physically in year of 2012 for the purpose of true, divine, eternally unconditional Twin Flame love, fulfilling their divine mission at the soul level.

Moreover, all combinations of Twin Flame unions (male/female, male/male, and female/female) are uniting and co- creating for the good of humanity and the planet. Therefore, whether it is a physical union or spiritual union, it is all-powerful.

It is because of December 21, 2012, that this planet reached another dimension. During this transmutation, many Twin Flame unions emerged. There was certainly no discrimination when it came to this emergence. These unions could be of the opposite sex or the same sex, all coming together in human form. Some may have gaps in age difference, a difference of religion, and geographical distances.

There will also be some Twin Flames, in Soul Mate unions while being in direct connection with their Twin Flame. This allows all parties involved to give and receive unconditional love and happiness for those Twins that may be involved in another relationship, as love rises between them all.

When you have opened your mind, body, soul, and spirit to embrace the universal energy love portals of ascension, you will become part of Earth's most important event in its history—

This is truly our Garden of Eden; our Heaven right here on Earth!

'Ascension'. All love given is love shared with all through our collective good. It brings to light the foundations of separation—that we have been living in—surpassing it by expanding our hearts bringing forth this divine love into the world. We hold in our vibrational escrow the unconditional love that which we all were created from. This uniting is an unfolding for us to expand through it, see it, feel it, and remember what this miraculous new evolution for humanity truly is. The Twin Flame union is not at all physical Love, but an ascending, unconditional deep, eternal true love from the soul level of each of us. It is the awareness and recognition of the Twin, in whatever form, that this union and co-creation will manifest.

Nevertheless, in this union, your Twin Flame's embrace to the incarnation on the physical level depends on your soul's intention and mission in this lifetime. Twin Flames bring limitless passion into the world that influences the human condition through the expression of lovingness and love intellect.

It takes the internal sense of completeness to experience Twin Flameship in everyday life! So if you are sincerely ready, open and willing to be with your Twin Flame, listen to your inner guidance, channeling you as you vibrate toward your Twin, flowing in every moment, feeling the unconditional love resonating through every experience, every challenge, and every connection. As you get closer to your Twin Flames heart, you will begin to ascend into a higher vibration connecting you to this union of ultimate love, and as you transcend into a deeper alignment with your Twin Flame your heart's expansion takes place in an instant by being on the same vibrational frequency as your Twin Flame.

This unfolding of divine love will bring you closer together into eternal oneness. Twin Flame unions are essential to bringing the collective awareness into the truth that our connection is beyond direct communication of our physical-ness. These Unions are capable to love beyond the minds and their physical-ness. It is well beyond the tangible, physical matter of these avatars. Twin Flame unions are essential in bringing the healing of separation into the full vibration of unions.

The Ascending Love Zone of Twin Flames

Author:

The ascending love zone is opened, reuniting Twin Flames in apropos and divine time. Connecting with one another, being reborn and awakened to the many truths to the Divine I AM Presence, validating our Ascension on December 21, 2012…

…Accepting realization that we are a spark of God! It is because our flames that make this ascension truly a one-of-a-kind miraculous and unique experience.

This allows our Twin Flameship to channel through the ascension process of emotional healing, transmuting our energy, and ultimately transforming our lives with one another, sharing that connectedness with one soul. Our Twin Flame union is the essences to the healing of separation—sending it into the full vibration of lovingness. ***This is truly our Garden of Eden; our Heaven right here on Earth!***

There will never be a love more powerful than your Twin Flame. It is the balanced completion of the whole, the circle of oneness, the 'other part of you', eternally romancing you through the apparent un-faltering and unwavering universe. It is like a bolt of lightning, when two stormy clouds collide. Our Twin Flame union has made a joyful happening to our lives. —Unknown Author

It is the destiny of Twin Flames Unions to Ascend together through the Eternal Love Portal!

"Now that our ascension has begun, we are preparing to fulfill our Divine Mission together, to help raise the consciousness of humanity and the planet, through our collective energy acting upon our hidden intuition that love it the only answer, which binds us all into a collective good."

—*Dawn M. Bunch*

CHAPTER SEVEN

TWIN FLAME REUNION STAGES

Our reuniting allowed us to enter the Ascending Love Zone of a Twin Flameship Union…Accepting the realization that we are a "spark" of God.

1. **Spiritual Awakening**
2. **Testing**
3. **Crisis**
4. **The Matrix Messengers**
5. **Spiritual Yielding**
6. **Radiance**
7. **Harmonizing**

Stage 1: Spiritual Awakening

Characteristics:

Both Twins recognize one another at the soul level and feel as if they have met before. Mirrored events surround their union. Their heart chakras are opened and cleansed! Both souls have manifested

into a third unified energy. Both Twins experiences are an accelera-
tion of spiritual understanding through their ascension. The purpose
of the Spiritual Awakening Stage: To activate the memory of your
Twin Flame's life mission as each Twin is awaken to higher levels of
consciousness.

Stage 2: Testing

Characteristics:

The egoic mind of self-definition re-emerges at times. Old thoughts
die hard because of fear, karma, and self-limiting beliefs. One or both
Twins may attempt to fit the union into the old, logic love pattern as
it relates to their ego desires and learned belief systems. Disharmony
arises which brings on conflict.

Twin Flames begin to ponder on what they were taught to believe
about how unions are supposed to be and how their partner is supposed to be. This may become a controlled environment filled with
egoic thoughts and dominance. This creates a critical or suspicious
environment on how both Twins view each other. Boy, talk about
being tested!

The purpose of the Testing stage:

> ➤ To cause out dated mental concepts about relationships to rise
> to the surface to be cleared.

Stage 3: Crisis

Characteristics:

The crisis of the Twin is realizing that they must reject their egoic mind of self-definition and limiting thoughts and beliefs about *all* things regarding Love and Unions. When we refuse to embrace a higher expression of Love, this can lead to a crisis in the relationship of unwillingness and anxiety. Having a constant fear and sense of insecurity may offset receiving that higher expression of Love, all to your dismay. When these thoughts emerge, they are to be witnessed, talked about, and released.

Being present with any concerns or fears about Love and Unions allow those thoughts to emerge. Each of you becomes open and receptive to each other's thoughts and emotions. In spite of the fears, both Twins are connected through the Love portals of affirmations, forgiveness, happiness, harmony, and intimacy. These portals bridge together higher levels of consciousness into the energy vortex of both Twins.

The purpose of the Crisis:

> ➤ To provide opportunities for the healing of *self,* your Twin, and maturing of the mind, body, soul, and spirit.

Stage 4: The Matrix Messenger Stage

Characteristics:

There is one fear the human ego constantly fears—annihilation, or separation, of a Twin Flame Union. Instead of trusting Divine Love, such fear causes the pain body to rise up and old ego survival tactics of old emotional and mental patterns emerge. This brings about the conflict of anger, judgment, and separation. One or both Twins become emotionally and mentally over-whelmed by a created illusion from the pain body. It is a feeling of rejection or abandonment, an emotional pain that leads to withdraw by one or both Twins. They drive a wedge in all communication with each other. When this happens, and if both Twins do not come back through their original connection of Divine Love, it may lead to stepping outside the vortex of their divine Twin Flameship.

Each soul learns from, walking its own path and choosing through its own will.

The purpose of the Matrix Messenger Twin stage:

> ➤ To expand toward God for healing and growth of the spiritual body.

NOTE: Because of the seductive temptation to do battle with the ego, this temptation is very hard to resist and difficult for many to surrender that feeling of illusional power, which is why many Twins Flames never reach that place of Yielding, Joy, Peace and Harmony.

Keep in mind that there is no room for judgment in this divine pairing of Twin Flames. It is on a soul level*! Each soul learns from walking its own path and choosing through its own will.* Keeping pure, positive, loving thoughts will create a strong barrier of Divine Love for your Twin Flame Union and others around you. The Matrix Messenger Twin will not know about their divinity while living their everyday like in society. They will feel and appear like the average person, although they may have an innate way of pulling spiritual information without understanding why.

Love will always be the beacon to guide us on our journey toward ascension.

The Matrix Messenger Twin *(Curtis)* is allowed the space and freedom to choose to evolve at their own pace in their own way. At this stage, the frequency of compassion returns and maintains itself. In general, the Matrix Messenger Twin will generally have their own psychic abilities, but the real powers of their abilities are usually tucked away in their DNA, waiting to be unlocked by the Spiritual Yielding Twin.

Stage 5: The Spiritual Yielding Twin

Characteristics:

The direction and outcome of this union is yielding to God, trusting that all Twin Flame Unions are divinely protected. This must take place on the soul level, as both Twins must reach illumination in order to become harmonized with physical incarnation. Your thoughts must be in that perfect higher state of divine consciousness! The Spiritual Yielding Twin **(Dawn)** holds a heart space for their beloved—while fully exploring life on the way to becoming awakened and illuminated in the physical realm. This may be a time for the Spiritual Yielding Twin to channel Unconditional Love into art, music, writing, teaching, active service, or some other creative outlet. This Twin will usually be the consciousness of the union and will have the duty of awakening the other Twin to their divinity and spiritual power. This means the spiritual Twin will most likely be more psychic and will generally feel uncomfortable in society for the most part.

The Purpose of the Spiritual Yielding Twin stage:

> ➤ To help each soul release the egoic mind of self-definition, develop regular communication with God, and demonstrate their full trust in Source to do what is best and when.

Stage 6: Radiance

Characteristics:

When the egoic mind of self-definition is detached—God Source assumes your mind, body, soul, and spirit…your *all*. It becomes the manifestation of a complete spiritual awakening, arriving at one's fully awakened light of divinity.

This is the stage of the ultimate radiating divine love rather than a physical, emotional or romantic love—love is neither of these things. Love is however, a consciousness, it is always emerging from source; it is an eternal gift of light that we all were created from. ***Love will always be the beacon to guide us on our journey toward ascension.***

At this stage, the Spiritual Yielding Twins' emotional, mental, and spiritual bodies emerge. This also allows them to help others to become awakened. This also allows the new creative mind's creativity and healing to take place. When the Spiritual Yielding Twin is in acknowledgment of this divine light—her illumined consciousness becomes *all* love. Her mantra for such divine radiance is…love is the only answer!

The Purpose of the Radiance stage:

> ➤ To establish an outward flow of Unconditional and Divine Love through one's body on a vibrational level. It resonates an uplifting, enlightening and yet spiritual manifesto to humanity.

Stage 7: Harmonizing

Characteristics:

This is the moment when both Twins have become awakened! They come together in the avatar of their physical incarnation to embrace their renewed, advanced announcement of who they have become—divine energies, flowing into the new dynamic of their unified potential. Both Twins integrate fully into the third energy of unconditional love that permeates to others. This enables the opening of their own hearts, to circumnavigate lovingness and love intellect to love *all*—throughout the cosmos.

The Purpose of the Harmonizing stage:

> ➢ To fulfill their deliberate mission—radiating perfect harmony. Twin Flame relationships come into your life to help guide you. You become an expression of perfect harmony and loving vibrations—through the frequencies of unconditional love, showing mutual respect for all humanity.

...When the egoic mind of self-definition is detached...God Source assumes your identity anew—your mind, body, soul, and spirit...your all. It becomes the manifestation of a complete spiritual awakening, arriving at one's fully awakened light of divinity—that light inside of you! This is the stage of ultimate radiating divine love rather than a physical, emotional, or romantic love— it is neither of these things. This light of love is a consciousness, it is always emerging from source, rearing its head of beauty. It does this whether you are aware of it or not...

...This kind of love is an eternal intimate gift of light that we all were created from. This love will always be the bright light— the beacon that guides you on your journey toward ascension— fulfilling your divine mission...

CHAPTER EIGHT

SIGNS OF TWIN FLAMES

*How do you know if you have met your
twin flame? Well, by the signs!*

Here are some common **Twin Flame signs.**

- You meet in an unusual way and completely by surprise.
- Instant recognition
- The feeling as though there is no passing time since you last saw them and yet it is the first time you met in this life.
- Their presence alone gives you a sense of completeness and security with an unshakable vibration.
- Communicate without words better than anyone else you know.
- Having been in the presence of your Twin, they never seem to leave your mind.
- This is the Holy Spirit energy flowing through your chakras.
- Experience of eyes going back and forth through eternity, like the infinity of two mirrors in front each other.
- This may feel like a vibrational shift in energy that you "transferred" to each other through your eyes.

- Dreams of them often in a silhouette shaped as two triangle halves joined as one.
- Dreams of a shadow of this person whose face you cannot visualize.
- The feeling that you never been fully illumined until you met them.
- Feeling you can truly be yourself around them with sincerity and that you cannot lie to them, nor they to you.
- There is no need to structure this Divine Union! It just *IS* from the very moment that you met.
- You feel a deep sense of sacredness in your spirit and closeness to God with them.
- There is an instant sense of trust and the holding of conversations can go on forever. Together you feel the deepest attraction and love for each other that does not waver.
- You suddenly begin to yield to an awakening spiritually and your life seems to grow and expand.

The term Twin Flame is becoming more knowledgeable in the metaphysical realm, especially the number of Twin Flame Unions that reunited during the December 21, 2012 Winter Solstice called "Ascension." This event took place to help raise awareness in the world—to awaken us through its unconditional and eternal love for life and all of humanity. It is the exceptional energies and power generated by Twin Flame reunions becoming more in existence today. Twin Flames have become the avatars manifesting together in greater numbers now with the special purposes of helping to maintain joyfulness, protect, and expand their energies, to move our world forward in preparation for the moments ahead.

Dawn and Curtis' Twin Flame Signs

Author:

"As it was stated earlier in the book, a Twin Flame is literally the 'souls' other half. It was the separation that occurred before entering 11:11—the dimension of consciousness.

We acknowledged our mirror image through third dimensional experiences derived from human incarnation in the physical and spiritual realm. Until recently, Twin Flame halves did not incarnate at the same time, but took turns supporting each other through respective human lifetimes. Curtis and I are certainly divine rare Avatars of the divine number 11:11. We are each other's Divine Compliment… We are perfect harmony—and it is our ultimate destiny to ascend together. We share mirrored life experiences as stated earlier in illustration chart on page 21 at the beginning of this book."

Here are some attributes of our Twin Flame Union:

1. **Having dreams or visions of this person, and/or your energetic union before ever meeting in this lifetime.**

2. **Meeting one another felt like "coming home" to a familiar, long-lost energy source.**

3. **We had mirrored issues, concerns, and imbalances, and yet we complemented each other's skill sets, talents, and capacities. We are the ultimate embodiment of yin/yang.**

4. **Dawn was the one of higher frequency, a First Waver** *(ridiculously domesticated)*, **Indigo (our crown chakras' open) and/or Crystal (my mythical birthstone, a diamond).**

5. **We are of different ages, similar backgrounds, "opposing" religions but we feel an incredible unity or incomparable sense of oneness with each other.**

6. **We feel each other's symptoms, illnesses, and emotions even when we may be apart from each other.**

7. **At times, our functioning is impaired or much less optimal when we are apart. It physically and mentally hurts when we are not together.**

8. **Our Twin Flame Union is in balance. We become stronger, more powerful, and more capable than we have ever felt. We feel united in a mission or "calling" to serve humanity and the world.**

9. **Our unconditional love for each other is like no other. We may have a certain habit, quality, or "baggage" that would be a deal-breaker in any other relationship. However, we overlook it and are always willing to work through it no matter what it takes.**

10. **When Curtis and I met, we were both involved in unions that made us "unavailable to be together at that moment. When we met, it was not a conscious expectation.**

11. **No matter how many times we had broken up or separated, "signs" and reminders of our twin connection were everywhere, urging us to get back together.**

12. **Our relationship is characterized by extreme highs and lows, including passion and intense pain, one of us most likely never felt before.**

13. **In our efforts to harmonize, justify, clean up our karma, and balance each other, we may "push each other's buttons" and test each other's limits like no one else has or ever will. Nevertheless, the extreme highs in this union consistently get higher.**

14. **Friends, family members, and others in our circle could not relate to the Twin Flame dramas and would at times try to get us to move on to someone or something else that seemed more logical or better than each other "on paper."**

15. **The expansion that we experience, the lessons we learn, and the persons we have become in this Twin Flame Union, is more significant, happens more rapidly, and is more powerful than any other experience or period of growth in our lives.**

16. **We have acknowledged that our previous soul mates or other relationships prepared us for our Twin Flame reunion.**

17. **As Twin Flames, we may even have or embody a number of the unusual characteristics or outstanding attributes of our previous mates and soul friends.**

18. **We feel as if we have been waiting our whole life for each other. When we look back at our life, we see illnesses, unbalanced relationships, or other situations that manifested because we were still awaiting and looking for "the one".**

19. **The more that Curtis and I spend time together, the more rapidly and completely awakened we are to higher consciousness.**

20. **We have a deep knowing that as Twin Flames, we are each other's destiny—not just in this lifetime, but also when we ascend, return "home", and reunited for eternity.**

Last but Not Least...The Dance

Resolving what is known as the Negative Karmic Connection

After having been in a relationship with your Twin Flame for a while, all the negative Karma emerges. As this may be a difficult process to go through at the physical level, it is actually a truly divine process. Both Twin Flames are cleansed in mind, body, soul, and spirit. They are in constant expansion with understanding and compassion that comes from the soul level, not physical. This lets them achieve higher energy levels so that they can ascend in bliss together.

This is also the phase where both Twin Flames get spiritually enlightened...This is when they, together, search and find the spiritual truth. If you are currently in a Twin Flame relationship, you are probably in this phase. *(This is the period when you usually begin finding out about your true self)*. Sometimes, it is not pretty! There will be much resistance due to the negative Karmic build-up over time. Moreover, when there is resistance, there is dis-harmony, disagreements and hurt. It all comes from—that's right, your negative Karma! It is best to get it up, get it out, and get it gone. Negative Karma has no place in your I AM Presence!

Arguments/Fights

Living with your Twin Flame can be very challenging at times. It is almost as though you are living with the other you.

The emerging negative Karmic connection between Twin Flames brings many arguments and fights. This happens because the negativity that each partner is carrying within comes to surface *(usually at a subconscious level)*. The Twin Flame will reflect this like a mirror and so you will think it is in them, when in reality, it is within you. Either this begins the deep cleansing process toward the harmony of Twin Flames because of the deep-rooted Karma; they never get to the level of Ascension and Surrendering.

In relationships nowadays, it's much easier to point the finger and walk away rather than to just ignore the ego and find out whether you are Twin Flames or not. When it feels off all the time you constantly clash. So, in a sense you are not Twin Flames. When you feel off in a relationship the ego *(pain body)* causes a serious discord and dis-harmony in relationships, even in a Twin Flameship. Yes, we are challenged too!

After an intense argument, the accumulated karma that has been buried for thousands of years becomes a whirlwind, revealing its ugly little head. The beauty of the beast is when the negative Karmic connection is released it is transmuted into Love.

Twin Flame energy is like a burst of Light illuminating Love.

This is essential in the last incarnation of Twin Flames as these deep-rooted connections, must be released, and must be transmuted, in order for the soul to move to another level of existence.

Only your Twin Flame pulls out all that negative Karma deeply rooted inside you…this long awaited emergence, bearing a resolution. This is a truly divine process that Twin Flames go through because they are cleansing each other and removing all underlying energies that are not of love. The conventional conscious mind may not grasp the deep meaning of this divine process regarding these arguments and fights among Twin Flames. Quite naturally, it would bring about much confusion and doubt if you are not aware.

The Blame Game

You begin blaming your Twin Flame for making you feel off all the time…In reality, it is not your Twin Flame or the arguments that make you feel inadequate; but rather a build-up of karmic residue that you are releasing. Your Twin Flame is only doing what they were created to do—to help bring it out on the surface to deal with it head on. Remember, get it up, get it out, and get it gone!

Typically, the human mind is not aware of karmic connection on a conscious level and unaware of what is happening. This divine work is something that only a Twin Flame does with great intensity. Other people and karmic relationships do help us release some of these build-ups, but a Twin Flame really is responsible for provoking them all forcing the egoic residue to come up and out. This causes much confusion in the mind. Your thoughts may be that your Twin Flame is making you feel *off*. When, in fact, it is really you. ***Twin Flame energy is like a burst of light illuminating Love.*** It washes away all that is not love from your very essence. In order for the negative

Karma to become detached, it has to first reveal itself, and become visible and washed away.

Keep in mind that the average conventional thinker will doubt this truly divine sacred Love. It is because the thought of love is someone who loves you and can never make you feel inadequate or off, which is not the case in Twin Flame Love. Noted, that this Twin Flame's love is the deepest that there is—not only on earth, but also in the entire universe. This is your other self who cleanses you from deep within, a place where no other can ever reach the way that your Twin Flame can. Your soul knows this because; your spirit is always guiding you! The average mind does not understand it, especially while it is happening, making it very upsetting, and confused.

This is the reason that people say a Twin Flame relationship is, the most difficult of any relationship. However, this can be the most beautiful, wondrous, happy union on the planet!

Author:

"Twin Flamships can be quite difficult—constantly releasing that *stuff* of thousands of years, the negative karma from within you…But know that this part of this Divine Sacred Twin Flame relationship ultimately benefits both of you. This is something that my Third Eye Chakra revealed to me, because I could not figure out for the life of me why we argue over the smallest things. Each Twin Flame sees their own negative *Karma* and *stuff* in their Twin Flame. They are not aware of the deep-rooted fears and frustrations that come to the surface. You start to think it is happening because of the other and start blaming each other. You might not realize it, but this is clearing all your *stuff*, which is a good thing." The arguments and the blaming cause a lot of discord, confusion, resistance, hurt and frustration. Usually, the spiritual process is not understood by the conscious mind, as we are conditioned to trust this way of thinking. The Yielding Twin normally is the first to surrender because of their higher, spiritual connection with *self*, the Universe, and God. The Messenger Twin responds to this high vibration of surrender in their own time.

The Preparation for your Twin

You must be open and receptive to the possibilities that your Twin Flame indeed does exist. Are you willing to prepare your mind, body, soul, and spirit for your Twin? Preparation must take place before meeting your Twin Flame. One of the main preparations is a past relationship that you may have been involved in that just was not meant to be for whatever reason. Here you have the negative karmic relationships, that void and strong desire.

Negative Karmic Relationships

There are many seriously devastating relationships in this world. They begin with strong emotions and end with much hurt and pain… They are Negative Karmic relationships.

First the Void and then that Strong desire for 'The Right One'

After you have been through negative Karmic relationships, you will have a very deep yearning or desire to find '*That Right One*'. At this point, you will desire meeting your perfect love, whose image you will carry in your imagination (or in some cases in dreams). This Image is of your Twin Flame, but you may not realize it at that time. This desire occurs because your soul knows that your Twin Flame is coming!

The Encounter is Heaven Sent

This is the phase when you meet your Twin Flame for the first time (in this incarnation). You might try to resist at this point but you will fall for him/her anyway. Then comes a short period of divine 'perfection' at its best, what I call, "Heaven Sent".

The Encounter

Author:

"When you meet your Twin Flame; your Divine Compliment, it is of unusual circumstance or it happens at some unexpected place like a Golf Course. I just know that having separated from my first husband; I never expected to meet anyone nor be involved in another long term relationship. His sentiments exactly! On a conscious level, neither one of us knew that this divine plan was for us to be in a Twin Flame union, but spirit never lies—it always knows the way. What we did notice at that point of our physical connection was that we both had a passion for golf.

At this point in your Twin flame encounter, you will find this person to be unique, even though your thoughts may might not even think of them as a significant other. Hell, I had just gone through a separation! Had no idea that he was going through the same exact thing. We never really touch on our personal life until we began seeing each other. WOW!"

The Initial Attraction

Author:

"You might not be ready for a relationship (because of the negative karmic relationships that you have experienced) and so you begin to resist the unfolding. You become unavailable and nowhere to be found. After my encounter with Curtis, it was nearly a whole month before he connected with me by sending flowers to my job. As mentioned in the beginning of the book.

Nevertheless, divine order steps in! You will fall strongly in love anyway. Not in the physical, sense but spiritual. All in this short period it is of the most breathtaking relationships that you have and will ever experience.

After the beginning attraction, you will find yourself in a profoundly romantic relationship. It will seem impeccable in every possible way. You will find all that you desired in your significant other and much more. This is what the Twin Flame relationship is supposed to be like, well beyond what words can say. A Twin Flameship is what it becomes after you get through the problems that surface from your Karmic connection with each other.

And they paint it with the colors of Unconditional Love.

This short period makes you aware of the perfection of yourself and your Twin Flame, bringing back the memories that were always deep within you, sort of like a déjà vu! Already, you begin to feel the urgency to go through the next level of Twin

Flameship called the Reunion. (This level can get little tough to understand on the conscious level).

The Reunion

This is when the split soul becomes *One* again! This happens first at the level of the soul and then in the physical plane. Yes, that is when you create this sacred married, unless, as in rare cases your physical reunion is not a part of the plane). The reunion happens when both the partners are fully aware of their deep connection with spiritual reality.

Eternally Blissful and Being all UNCONDITIONAL LOVE!

When they say love is in the air, with Twin Flames, it is always there everywhere present in its totality. Both Twin Flames are spiritually awakened and enlightened. There is a perfect, peaceful, loving and harmonious union surging. The twin Flames together will now enjoy their sacred love and intimacy. They have the power to create whatever their desires are…The world becomes their canvas…***And they paint it with the colors of Unconditional Love.***

At the end of the Twin Flame journey on Earth, they ascend together and go on to experience more; just like they always have in other worlds and other planets. Within this universe is their *'sand box'* and beyond…Together, in eternal love, joy, peace, and harmony. Together, both Twin Flames are eternally blissful and complete.

(Are you willing to ascend with your Twin Flame)?

Now that you have gotten to this point, there is no sense in stopping now, is there? The question to ask yourself at this moment is, "Am I Ready to meet ME? Do you want to hear the answer? Sure you do! But if you are not ready then it is best to just put this book down. Now if you are ready to meet your *authentic crystalline self* then…you must continue and…

Keep…

…Reading!

CHAPTER NINE

MEETING YOUR TWIN FLAME, THE OTHER YOU!
MEETING YOUR TWIN FLAME, THE OTHER YOU!

Your Twin is with you completely in mind, body, soul, and spirit.

You are Yin and they are Yang rapped within each other; it is how God created you—exactly as Twin Flames would be. Everything you experience you share with your Twin Flame. It is impossible not to. There are no exceptions to this rule! Everything that you come into vibration with, you share it with your Twin Flame. As you become conscious of each other, things will become evident and you will experience nearly everything that your Twin Flame does.

So as you open your consciousness beyond the belief that things on Earth are solid, you will begin to share the experience of a glorious spiritual union. One in which the "I Am," is ever and fully present, in the both of you. Twin Flames must choose to send and receive their experiences to each

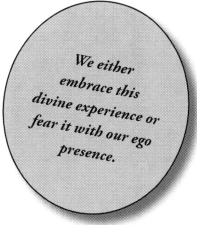

We either embrace this divine experience or fear it with our ego presence.

other. When they become open and receptive…true *love* comes! It will break down any thoughts of separation because *love* wants only the reunion with its Twin Flames.

You will come to know the love and beauty of each and every experience within each moment of this new awareness. You want to send them only love and beauty. This unfolding is love eternal and that you are in perfect condition for your good—to feel each precious moment, to see each day anew. It is the perfect opportunity to share each other's life as this union is not measured by egoic standards, but by the divine love of mirrored souls reunited.

The Many Faces of Your Ego Causes Distraction

Always remain in pure positive thought and stay in truth. It is through your heart chakra that the truth in everything you choose to be (of Love, of union and of openness), will guide you directly into contact with your Twin Flame heart. Together you are made of love and oneness. This truth of your Twin Flame union only happens through the *soul* and *heart*. In this case, be mindful in that everything of the ego you consciously choose or allow will actually obscure that love. This keeps discord and distraction between the two of you. When your egos are in battle, you become weaken and confused. Obstacles somehow find their way not only in your union but in your lives as well. It is really your consciousness reflecting how you do the work to live in love, joy, peace, harmony, happiness and well-being.

Author:

"There were moments in our union that Curtis and I were bound to go our separate ways because of what we did not understand. We were on the verge of just walking away from this Twin Flameship.

We were no receptive of the divine mission this union had instore for us. Our egos that stood in the way of this unfolding—not knowing that this Twin Flameship union was designed for us from the day of our creation. The energy from this divine source would not allow us to separate.

We have come to know that Twin Flames unions are indeed complicated at times, because we are a mirror image—we are in the presence of ourselves. ***We either embrace this divine experience or fear it with our ego presence.*** We chose to embrace it!

Now that we have come to embracing this divine Twin Flameship, we must stay on the path to fulfill our divine mission. Nothing can take us off the path because we are love eternal, we are always together, and we are always connected. There is nothing more powerful than this eternal Twin Flame love. Nothing can separate that! When you choose to Love in every moment and seeing the world only through your heart, you are in real direct contact with your Twin Flame, able to bathe in every moment of love and beauty of this divine union. When you give unconditional eternal love to yourself, it resonates within your Twin. Together, Curtis and I dismiss all our egoic idio-syncrasies and selfishness, with unconditional love, purity and ten-derness. In doing so, we love the world just as well.

When you love your Twin Flame unconditionally, you love your-self unconditionally! Your Twin is a reflection of you in every way, including any barriers that still lingers within. You must Love in truth through expression of who you really are. For in truth, it really is all you have. When you take the all-that-is and see it through the eyes of a Twin Flame, one of whom I was created to be, I have that perfect one. The one true love, the true and perfect heart of devo-tion, giving and sharing the Love I AM! Every moment we have the opportunity to dance through the orgasmic wonder of our Creation together. Each day as we ascend together as Twin Flames, we possess the gift of divine likeness, packaged with every golden moment of our existence. I know that throughout the course of your life, you had a few unusual or powerful dreams, premonitions, or fantasies of a mysterious person.

You have a vague feeling that this person is real even if you cannot see a face or even try to invent their physical appearance in your mind. There may have been a particular feeling and energy of this individual as if it is someone you have already met in the past or perhaps someone you will meet in the unknown future. You have a distinct feeling as if this person is out there somewhere waiting for you and may even know who you are on the same level. There may be an unusual feeling of co-existence or an event that surrounds that first initial meeting between Twin Flames.

Often, you have a feeling or 'intuitiveness' of something and you know it's there but you just can't quite put it into words. When Twin Flames often encounter each other for the first time, it is in an unusual way. A Twin Flame will come into your life in an unexpected way out of the blue. Usually there are strange occurrences that may cause major shifts in energy the same week of the initial encounter. You feel an overwhelming strong attraction; gravitating pulling you in.

This love is genuine and heartfelt and you feel magnetically drawn to their energy. This is not to be confused with lust or an obsessive love to fill a void. Twin Flame love is 'liking'— it is an unconditional love that supersedes the ego. If you have found your Twin Flame, it does not mean that the relationship will necessarily be free from issues or personal conflict *(stuff)*. There may still be lessons and healing that must take place between the Twin Souls due to your Karmic Connection. When you become aware that you are with your Twin, you will begin to feel a sense of blissfulness and completeness that goes beyond words.

This feeling is about wholeness on a soul level that is beyond all physical-ness. Each Twin Flame is still an individual, but becomes a complete connected soul having been reunited.

So in a sense, you are meeting the mirror image of your own soul. You share a vibration that permeates though you, like the nectar from a flower, carried in the wind. You even feel an attraction to the sound of their voice as it may even sound familiar to you as if you have heard it before. It is the soul that has attracted your Twin to you, not some happenstance!"

There is a Bond Beyond the Physical

You will complement one another on a high vibration that connects several aspects of your personality, outlook on life or mirrored idiosyncrasies that you both may share. But, since the both of you are unique individuals, there will be some differences. There will also be aspects of your Twin Flame that seem completely opposite to you. However, it is your individual traits and opposite qualities that are the very strengths and perceptions. This will help to balance out your Yin and Yang if ego is transcended. Twin Flames are connected on a soul level. Twin Flames are empathic with one another with a bond that goes beyond the physical. Even at a distance, Twin Flames often feel each other's vibration.

For example, if one is feeling depressed or ill the other may pick up on this energy and begin to feel the same. Twin Flames have the ability to feel each other's emotions, whether happy or sad, from great distances. Often times Twin Flames experience similarities in their energies that they may encounter during certain activities and events. It's as if they are always with one another, which mean they are in a spiritual and vibrational sense!

Twin Flames often know what the other is feeling or thinking even when the other hasn't said a word or is not thinking out aloud. It is because of this that Twin Flames often know if the other is deceiving them or keeping a secret. Often times it can be quite difficult to keep something from your Twin Flame because you both know and feel each other on a deep soul level and can see through the pretense of the ego and its illusions. There is usually an automatic honesty throughout the Twin Flame relationships.

It is as if you cannot hide from one another and there is often no need to remain in falseness of the ego for long. There is a desire to be authentic with the Twin Flame because you know each other on a level that again "goes beyond the physical." It is unconditional love, and genuine acceptance of each other's individuality that underlines the Twin Flame relationships.

This root foundation of authentic self-expression, unconditional love and honesty is essential for a Twin Flame relationship to remain harmonious during times of conflict and discord. The soul wants these tests for growth as these are opportunities for Karmic Connections to be resolved.

Like all relationships, Twin Flame couples will still experience issues. Often the drama can be more intense during disagreements but is often resolved more quickly! For example, Curtis and I have our disagreeable moments where we don't see eye to eye and compromise is a thousand miles away! So, when we cannot come to an agreement or compromise, we know how to go to that place that sparks—the day of our creation. We now are able to look at the situation with better eyes and a better understanding. We often pick up on each other's thoughts and sometimes even finish one another's sentences.

We find ourselves calling, emailing and texting one another at the exact same time. The phone could be ringing and before I pick it up I know it's my husband. This can happen more often during periods of our heightened energy or when we are in a similar vibration one day and very tuned in to each other energetically. The co-existence in the lives of the Twin Flames also occurs more often during these heightened periods of soul growth.

The Perfect Union, How Can This Be?

Love on the Soul Level

Go ahead and change your thoughts, by paying attention to the way you feel. I dare you to detach those old self-limiting beliefs, those old thoughts all coming from that negative Karmic connection.

Yes, this is what has attached itself to your very existence as you expand and evolve on this planet. This is what your ego strives for as it continues to be in control of mere illusions that you have surrounded your consciousness with.

Awakened to the ever-expanding Source Energy You!

You can detach your mind, body, soul, and spirit from your ego constantly giving you an illusion that hurt, pain and rejection is your comfort zone. Detaching yourself from this untruth is just like turning a light switch on and off. It can be done in an instance. Sometimes, it can take longer, but not too much longer. It cannot co-exist with the desire to meet your Twin Flame.

It is the fear of meeting your true, authentic *self*...that which you were created from...unconditional love. Negative Karma is not who you truly are. Yes, the many faces of your ego has manipulated your existence for thousands of years, hoping that you will not turn the other cheek—in other words, continue to be submissive to the illusions it presents to you. It is the shifting of ones' consciousness, yielding to the infinite possibilities of the all that is-ness. The unfolding to new awakening will turn the tables!

You will begin to experience your awakened spirit now in full control of your consciousness, all that you seek and desire… ***Awakened to the ever-expanding Source Energy You!***

It was twelve years ago that I yielded to a divine calling greater than life itself. I became open and receptive to those infinite possibilities that existed; they were already there. They existed through the Mind of God, through the Mind of Lovingness, through the Mind of Love Intellect, through the Mind of cosmic Universal Knowledge that is everywhere present in its fullness. I was ready for my true love, my Twin Flame, my Divine Compliment. That was *ME*! I was ready to meet *ME*! Being in acknowledgment of this awakened consciousness has brought me, my other half—my Twin Flame on a mental, physical, spiritual, and soul level. All of *me* had become awakened, enlightened, uplifted and happy.

YOU MUST BE WILLING, NOT JUST WILLING, EAGER, NOT JUST EAGER, TO MEET YOUR TRUE AUTHENTIC CRYSTALINE SELF.

> ➢ WHO IS YOUR TRUE LOVE?

> ➢ WHO IS YOUR TWIN FLAME?

> ➢ WHO IS YOUR DIVINE COMPLIMENT? ⌐→

∟→ YOU!

YOUR ARE ALL THAT IS!

YOU ARE THE...I AM PRESENCE!

YOU ARE THE LOVE I AM,
EVERY MOMENT!

YOU ARE THE MIRROR IMAGE OF *SELF*!

Author:

"One may find this hard to believe, but my husband Curtis and I have the PERFECT union. We realize that all disagreements and arguments all come from the past negative Karmic Connection. This kind of negative energy has a tendency to latch itself into our consciousness. It is throughout thousands of years does this energy when allowed, grows with expansion and evolution of mankind. This is not such a bad thing! When this kind of Karma emerges, it is for a reason: to bring it up, clear it out, detach it, and expand. Be mindful that the Ego creates many illusions to make one's consciousness think that you, your union and your life is headed for total destruction. It is just that Ego is always in control and *wanting to be in control. It fights to yield to our divine, paved path to complete our Divine Mission.*

Curtis and I have shifted our consciousness to a place that does not allow the co-existence of unconditional love and the ego. If something is off in our union, we bring it up, clear it out, and detach ourselves from it. We go back to that which has brought us together from the very beginning of our creation…Unconditional Love."

If you do not have a good relationship with yourself, you cannot expect to have a good relationship with anyone else…Especially your Twin Flame.

CHAPTER TEN

KEEPING THE HONEY IN THE MOON

KEEPING THE HONEY IN THE MOON

Intimate relationships are a powerful way
to anchor light into the planet.

Can We Play

The Twin Flame experience is only for those whom are ready to embrace their authentic crystalline *self*. That's right; take a good look in the mirror! Are you ready for YOU? The Twin Flame relationship is the most ultimate challenge on Earth as it exposes the ego's core of illusions.

A Twin Flame relationship is not about who's right or wrong, peaches and cream, nor is it a field of daisies! It is the sharing of the soul being in constant joy and harmony no matter what each moment may bring.

The ultimate goal here is in the long-term outcome—to become blissful and complete! It is the passion of Twin Flames sharing at the very deepest of levels. Their bodies, their lives, their breath, their thoughts and opening their hearts. Their spirits merge as they transmute in divine love. This is a divine marriage on a soul level and nothing can destroy this union. It is the Twin Flame chemistry that creates an almighty vortex through which Divine Love flows as it anchors into the Earth's plane.

When the relationship gets to this stage, and deservingly so, it is highly praised due to the individual divine work that is well under way by both Twins as *One*. This becomes the result of all previous shared life experiences—of two Christ consciousness *beings* joined as *One*. This is the reality of the incarnation of two physical bodies sharing one soul manifested on Earth. It was a divine mission to make a difference. This mission is to help raise the consciousness of humanity and the planet. It is the aiding of co-creation and bringing newness within personal relationships. This awareness allows the creative mind to bring all that we desire; serving all humanity.

Therefore, we all can live a harmonious and peaceful life. Keep in mind that Twin Flame relationships are incredibly creative. They physically mirror themselves almost instantaneously. Twin Flames have diverse streams of thoughts that are magnified. It is important that the two Twin lovers be harmonized *as one*—with an aligned focus of shared goals.

The intimacy of the Twin Flame relationships is untouchable and should be honored as such. They worship the creative God and Goddess in each other. In doing so, this love can be taken out into the world to lift up Earth's vibrations and move any darkness away. This is how to change the world—by making LOVE. When the moon's energy flows, it will radiate! The oceans' tides rise and fall. Flowers will grow and blossom all during the time of your orgasm. It will all flow together through this true Twin Flame union.

As your bodies explode forth in orgasmic ecstasy and you are Making Love with your Twin Flame in heart and consciousness, it is a gift to every cell to join you in the Moment of Creation. To those who are a stone throw from their Twin Flame for whatever reason, have the advantage of learning to love, or to make love from sifting through your buffet. Those past relationships prepare you for the meeting of your Twin Flame. Although they are apart, Twins will spend time joining in conscious love making through their heart chakras. They allow the real love making experience to attract everything within their consciousness...

Together, they partake in a breathtaking orgasmic *now*—that sacred place! When the moment arrives for Twin Flames to be together in this world, it will be their Love Making Conscious Connection. This brings all parts of their beings into the ultimate orgasmic union of the heart and consciousness!

Always in the Moment...
...Setting the Mood with Music

It is said that music soothes the savage beast inside of us! It does one thing! It brings out the true intimate passion that you have always possessed.

There is nothing wrong with expression through song and dance in front of your Twin Flame, or for that matter, your significant other. It is certainly ok to express yourselves during the most sacred and truest moments that the two of you stand before. Ladies, it is ok to stand in the doorway while your significant other turns the key, comes in, and finds you standing there barefoot, or in a pair of stilettos, naked wrapped up in a fur coat. Whatever provocative garment of your choice! Oh and men, it is ok to stand at the door when she walks in posing like the Renaissance Man.

Twin Flame Love is ageless and timeless!

Whatever your choice, you are keeping the *"Honey in the Moon!"* You are making it fun, passionate, and intensifying this moment of your sacred union. There is nothing wrong with it! In fact, I encourage you to do it as often as you can. Yes, making love, being a little on the wild side, feeding that fire will explosively enhance this passionate intimate moment of a consciousness and physical energy exchange.

Author:

"My husband Curtis and I acknowledge that our connection of intimacy comes from the soul and not from the physical plane. Wherever we are, this vibration of passion never misses a beat! When the moment of intimacy comes calling, we yield and surrender to the vibration of intimacy and ecstasy stepping into the Twin Flame Love Portal. As Twin Flames, our intimate moments are far more intense than that of those who are not in a Twin Flame union. When you keep the 'Honey in the Moon' the Honeymoon never ends!"

This kind of energy resonates from this seductive, passionate and appealing music that sends the mind, body, soul, and spirit into that dynamic love vortex—our DANCE!

Twin Flame Love is ageless and timeless! The burning passion and desire is not about bodies; it is about the souls dancing together to the intimate harmonious beat of Lovemaking. It will be our work to reunite these glorious Twin Flames in truth, in heart and consciousness, and then to bring them close in their bodies. As you first attune yourselves together through your hearts chakra, you will experience the ecstasy of who you really are…Pure love on all levels.

This is real not a fantasy. Beloveds, you must allow your bodies to join in the Love. Allow every cell from the atoms of which you are made from, to join and return with you to the orgasmic 'moment of creation'. Allow the moment within this union to become embraced by every fiber of your *being*. When Twin Flames intertwine they begin to share the most intimate space within this sacred journey—everything around them is also making love.

Take everything of love and beauty, see it with the eyes of your Twin Flame, one whom was created with you and for you, to be the perfect lover, the true and perfect heart of devotion, and the giving of Unconditional Love that you are. With every moment, you have the opportunity to dance through the orgasmic wonder of creation together. Every day is a gift of golden moments, each one waiting for you to notice and send as a gift to your Twin Flame.

Therefore, Beloveds, ask yourselves:

ARE YOU REALLY KEEPING THE HONEY IN THE MOON?

WHAT IS DETERRING YOU FROM KEEPING THE HONEY IN THE MOON?

SUGGESTION!

GO OUTSIDE YOUR COMFORT ZONE! BOTH OF YOU JUST MIGHT LIKE!

It is the soul's connectedness of Twin Flame love that infuses their heart chakra. It creates the ultimate vibration for intimacy. Lovemaking is the ultimate expression of this union. The bond between Twin Flames can be so intense, that during lovemaking the connection alone is sufficient satisfaction rather than having a pure orgasm. Twin Flames can be apart and yet feel that level of extreme sexual vibration to that of a 'mating' call. Only with your Twin Flame—are they receptive to this vibrational calling, especially under the lunar moons, which amplifies that energy.

—Dawn M. Bunch

Author:

I would send my husband a text at work every now and again, and this is what I would say to him:

*"Our union is a beautiful song and dance. I admire you,
Husband, and see greatness in you. I see the divine light
of Spirit shining within you. Together we walk as Twin
Flames on our destined path. What a great job you are
doing! I am so proud of you! I place you in the loving light
of Spirit. You are my hero. I am here waiting Beloved!"*

His response is, "On my way!" ;-)

Now that is one way to keep the honey in the moon!

When your bodies are in alignment together, you will experience
the intensity of not just the physical-ness of lovemaking, but a spiritual
intensity. The flame of love is turned up warming the soul. You can
literally feel each other's thoughts, emotions, and desires. It is a burning passion of ecstasy, beyond any expression of such DEEPNESS in
the moment. You have now entered into the Vortex of Love. It is the
true expression of love, a transmutation of divine love through each
touch, each word, and each look. Just *being* next to each other in the
physical presence sends intense waves of energy throughout the entire
body. You become enlivened as all of the chakras are opened. It is two
divine vessels receiving and being in love with one another, sending
the vibrational frequencies of this spiritually divine love for each other
out into the universe.

*"No matter where you are in the world, when we display our
divine love and affection for each other, we are indeed fulfilling
our divine mission; bringing unconditional love to the world."* ~
—**Dawn M. Bunch**

**SO GO AHEAD BELOVEDS, EXPRESS YOUR LOVE AND
AFFECTION FOR THE ENTIRE WORLD TO SEE!**

It is when you resist the urgency and the willingness to give love and affection to each other do you limit yourselves from evolving and expanding within the essence of your *beings* which is totally responsible for giving unconditional love to all.

<u>WHO IS UNCONDITIONAL LOVE?</u>
GOD IS!

<u>WHAT IS UNCONDITIONAL LOVE?</u>
IT IS THE ABSOLUTE ALL-EMBRACING
AQUIESCENCE OF WHAT IS!

<u>WHAT DOES UNCONDITIONAL LOVE DO?</u>
IT MOVES ALL THINGS!

Dawn and Curtis' Sacral Chakras are open!

What about Yours?

Take the three-minute Charka Test with Carol Tuttle
and find out where you stand with your Chakra's.
www.**chakra**healing.com/**ChakraTest**

Music for the Intimate Dance

Curtis and Dawn's Playlist:
The River (Santana)
Forevermore (Enchantments)
You're the Best Thing In My Life (Dramatics)
If Anything Ever Happen To You (Bee&Cee Winans)
I'm Back For More (Al Johnson & Jean Carne)
Just Because (Anita Baker)
Priceless (Anita Baker)
You're the Best Thing Yet (Anita Baker)
Soul Inspiration (Anita Baker)
Just My Imagination (Temptations)
Stay (Temptations)
This Is My Promise (Temptations)
To Be Continued (Temptations)
Unchained Melody (The Righteous Brothers)
The Last Time I Made Love (Jeffrey Osborne & Joyce Kennedy)
Let Me Know (Jeffrey Osborne)
Crazy 'Bout Cha (Jeffrey Osborne)
Lovers Everywhere (Jeffrey Osborne)
Love Ballad (Jeffrey Osborne)
Won't Cha Stay With Me (L.T.D)
All The Way Around (Marvin Gaye)
Since I Had You (Marvin Gaye)
With Open Arms (Rachelle Ferrell)
Nothing Has Ever Felt Like This (Rachelle Ferrell)
Love All The Hurt Away (Aretha Franklin and George Benson)
Flame Of Love Turn It Up (Jean Carne)
2 AM (Teddy Pendergrass)

Baby I Need Your Love Today (Sweet Thunder)
You Make Love Like Spring Time (Teena Marie)
It's Our Anniversary (Tone, Toni, Tony)
Ebony Eyes (Rick James & Tina Marie)
A Rainy Night In Georgia (Brook Benton)
I Can Make It Better (Luther Vandross)

Hey, if you do not feel like dancing, you can just sit at home and watch a movie, watch sports, or watch each other. Never mind that the kids are at home…Spontaneity adds the fire to those flames you know. So why not play a little before they come up, down, or in your space. Now that is keeping the Honey in the Moon! If your kids come running in on you, play it off and act as if nothing even happened. You know that's what some of you do anyway! Oh, but they will give you this, "What yawl doing; look?" Well, you know what to say! "Oh nothing, we're just sitting here watching television." Kids will hold you to that story and then make themselves comfortable right there with you! You have to love it! We know how to come up with something quick! You pre-plan and already know what to say to kids! However, in the meantime, enjoy each other's company!

As for the intimacy, it keeps the honey in the moon…

CHAPTER ELEVEN

IT WAS JUST NOT MEANT TO BE

IT WAS JUST NOT MEANT TO BE

*Allow yourself to Sift through your "buffet in the
sand box", just like kids in an ice cream shop! There
is a buffet of flavors to choose from; trying new
flavors until they have found the one they love.*

Exes, don't Take It Personal…
No One Is to Blame

All of your past unions prepared you for your Twin Flameship. It is
because you are now open and receptive to the possibilities. You
allowed yourself to sift through your buffet without judging any of
it. You may not care for Prime Rib, but found yourself preferring
Lobster. You may not care for apple pie, but find yourself liking cherry
pie! Now this is where the sifting comes into play here.

Let's say that you have been sifting through your buffet and playing in your sandbox. You may not care for what it is you are tasting
and things feel off to you. Well, don't just sit there and be unhappy
with sand thrown all over you. It is okay to tell the person you have
been with for twenty or two years that the union feels off. You do not
want to play in the "sand box" anymore! If your happiness is being

neglected, it is because of *you* and what you are not bringing to your table of consciousness.

The sincerest question to ask yourself is, "Why be in a union where there is NO HAPPINESS, NO PEACE, NO HARMONY? Oh, I see; you're doing it for the kids, the cat, the dog, your mom, your dad, your social status. Here is something else that you are doing—yielding to the egoic mind of self-definition—a mere illusion.

I will say that this is all of what you are attracting! You deserve to have sand thrown all over you! Why not do what is best for YOU? Ok, so you want to try to work it out! Go for it! Hey, you might find yourself on a hamster wheel constantly running a circle around the illusions of false premise. This is what you are attracting and the same goes for your significant other. You may just have to come to the realization that he/she is not the one for you. They are not your Twin Flame!

Now here comes the hard part. You know…that part you do not want to be accountable for. DENIAL! Well, there it is…Yes I said it! Now what are you going to do about making YOU happy? Sometimes, relationships just do not work out! They just are not meant to be! It could be that either one is not happy within themselves, with that person or their relationship. You are not the one…Oh, but don't take it personal exes!

Be with your Twin Flame and Love like a child playing in the "Sand Box!"

Author:

"Relationships are supposed to prepare you for the meeting of your Twin Flame…The ultimate love of your life! I am almost certain that my husband and I are not the only Twin Flames experiencing an extraordinary Twin Flameship. I am sure that many couples can relate to the "MIRROR IMAGE" 11:11 story. The great thing about this book is that it is not just for those in Twin Flame unions, but for those seeking to be with their other half also known as your "Divine Compliment."

There are those who may be just starting out yearning to be with their Twin Flame. Some may be getting out of toxic unions, some may be waiting for that Twin Flame to show up, and some just want 'new age' ideas to add upgrades to their harmonious union. Well, what are you waiting for?

Get up out of the "sand box" full of dis-harmony, illusions and toxins. Dust yourself off and take a good hard look at your *"BUFFET"* of what you get to pick and choose from. You must allow the unfolding to take place in order for you to have a peaceful, happy, and harmonious union with *self-*first. Then do what YOU *(a radiant being of light),* were created to do…LOVE. Yes, you were created from the LOVE! All creation comes from it!

Okay, now that you have experienced the tasting of your choice of what was served to you, be grateful for those tasting experiences and find a better sand box. ***Be with your Twin Flame and Love like a child playing in the "Sand Box!"*** You get to choose what you want in your 'buffet' and you get to play in the new "sand box!

The Illusion of False Premise Love Contract

Your previous or past unions were contracts to help prepare you to be with your Twin Flame. So, to all of the Ex-Husbands, Ex-Wives, Ex-Lovers, Ex-Boy Friends and Ex-Girl Friends, it just was not meant to be. Know that it's okay! We are ever expanding for our greater good; that's a good thing! You were part of a journey that included you for a moment! Be grateful for those experiences that you once shared—good, bad, or indifferent. You will begin to expand when you let go of old grudges, old baggage, old garbage, and old karma.

True, unresolved feelings of rejection are embedded, keeping you from yourself and from any truths that you may feel. So why not remove yourself from your disharmonizing circumstances and embrace yourself fully for no reason other than you always have a choice. You value your love and honor the new friendship you have within yourself.

Sometimes, we allow ourselves to fall into situations that we do not intentionally put ourselves in. Often times those situations are negative. Those situations are experiences and when you become grateful for them, you will find peace within. When you forgive in all moments, you will find a lasting choice of love in friendships that benefits you and the other person. They connect to you in honesty. The honesty of truth will always be with you it never leaves! This is not a fear that will keep you from making or finding new places inside you…In fact it opens the door to always allow your love to be placed inside of the space that is truly and deeply within yourself.

The Toxicity of the False Premise

I can tell you right now that the majority of relationships were toxic, are toxic, and will be toxic. Why do I say this? It was a false premise from the very beginning. Now all this toxic stuff infiltrated your psyche and those in your circle, absorbing the residue from your dis- harmonizing relationship. It was toxic because you allowed it to be. You allowed your egoic mind of self-definition to resonate and be in control. It is within the pain body that creates this false premise, and you believe it. There is much dis-harmony and discord going on! When your relationship becomes toxic, everyone around you gets a taste of it and it is difficult to shake a loose.

Yes, there is a whole lot of negative Karmic Connection going on in your appearance of illusory relationship. One of you is zigging and the other is zagging. Why is the sand box no longer fun to play in! Only you have the answer!

No you're not crazy or losing your mind!

Would you like to find out why your relationship is toxic? It's very simple… Because it is… How do you expect to have a loving, blissful, harmonious, and peaceful relationship when it is based on toxic false premises? The fact that you are with someone and knowing that the whole relationship is off. You're not clicking, you're not on the same page, you're not on the same vibrational frequencies. Then there is all this, infidelity, abuse and loss of respect for love and life for yourself and others. The result of why a relationship loses its natural luster; its connectedness, is because there was nothing natural about it to begin with! Ever heard of physical infatuation?

Well I am here to tell you to your FACE! It is nothing but a mere illusion! It is no wonder that many relationships end in divorce and separation. There is no connection on the vibrational, soul and spiritual level in your relationship...there never was. In spite of what your inner guidance, your intuitive nudge is telling you on a subconscious level..."You know it's not right!" You feel it with every fiber of your being and still you stay in it. Yes, I am talking about that voice that you hear every so often. ***No you are not crazy or losing your mind!*** It is true about what they say about the voices inside of you chattering. Be mindful of the chatter though...It's the good chatter that moves your intuitive nudges always guiding you toward your greatness to be—leading you on the right path to happiness and well-being.

Keep in mind that it is your intuitive voice from that higher place always telling you when something is good for you or that something is off. When you feel good through good intensions, it feels good to you right? But, when it does not feel good and it is with bad intentions, it feels off; it feels bad to you. If it feels genuinely good from that light, from the soul, from every fiber, then it is right for you! If it feels off, then it is not right for you! This is called non-compatibility!

It's like trying to fitting a round peg into a square hole. Hey, there are some out there to make it fit! How? By beating it, disfiguring it, putting dents and bruises on it. Hey, guess what, when it goes into that square, it is stuck, with no room for movement or change. Are you hearing this? Well! Are you? If you have allowed my words to guide you through this book and you have gotten to this point...Can you *HEAR THE ANGLES SINGING FOR YOU*? Now you are well on your way to discovering your true self and your Twin Flame. But if you choose to end it here, so be it!

Your unequally yoked relationships are on a hamster wheel and instead of expanding in a peaceful harmonious oneness, you let that wheel steer you into relational discord and dis-harmony.

Look at the illustration chart 1-3, on page 121 that will tell you where you are in your union or relationship and what to do to get on the left side and stay there.

Ok, let's look at what makes a relationship to be either harmonious, toxic or a mere illusion:

Illustration Chart 1-3

Are you here?	OR	Are you here?
Compatible		Unsuited
Joy		Sadness
Happiness		Discontent
Peacefulness		Anxiety
Harmonious		Discordancy

Compatible

"There is a special bond between Divine Compliments—sharing one soul, divine connectedness, unconditional love, mutual respect for each other, bringing out the best in each other; they are highly compatible." —Dawn M. Bunch

That which is 'liking' is drawn!

When you develop the sense of desire for the same likeness that is within you the universe receives it through your vibrational frequencies. The universe then responds and it brings to you that which is liking. We are drawn into each other's creations through compatible (like) desires, wants and needs. This "like attracts like" action is a mere expression of the Law of Attraction.

Unsuited

Often times there are those voices inside your head that speak to you. They are your sane voice and your chatter voice. Stop listening to the chatter…Listen to the sane. You are in control!

That 'sane' voice tells you that sooner or later, you are going to have to be honest with yourself and just say, "I don't want to play in the sand box anymore!" It just was not meant to be!

It's called being in an 'unequally yoked' union. He's zigging and she's zagging. When you *feel* that you are headed for a collision, in your relationship—then your intuitive nudge is precisely correct. It's basically what you have been attracting all your life, are still attracting and will continue to attract if you do not change what you think about! Remember, you are what you think about all day long—thoughts become things! Why this incompatibility? You are not on the same vibrational frequency, that spells unsuited…You are both in denial! What gets in your way is the feeling that you owe someone something. Why stay if that sane voice inside your head is telling you that it just is not meant to be. So why not listen to the good chatter and do what is best for YOU? You do have a choice; you are not obligated to be in a relationship that breeds discord.

Joy

Joy is a return to the deep harmony of body, mind, and spirit that was yours at birth and that can be yours again. That openness to love, that capacity for wholeness with the world around you is still within you." —Deepak Chopra

What is above love? It is joy, peace, and enlightenment. The basis of your life is freedom; the purpose of your life is joy. You are free to choose and discover new avenues of joy. In your joy, you will grow and add to the growth experience of all-that-is.

Joy is an essential spirit practice. It is the growing of our faith, grace, gratitude, hope, and love. It is a pure and simple delight in being alive. Joy is an elated response to feelings of happiness, experiences of pleasure and awareness of abundance. It is an internal state of consciousness, which will determine how you perceive and experience the world. This source of joy is your connection to God Source and your inner self—your happiness is its effect.

Sadness

*"The walls we build around us to keep sadness out also keeps out the joy." —***Jim Rohn**

Sadness is a natural feeling which, if unfelt, just lingers in our consciousness of unresolved (*karmic connection*) that I call *stuff*. When you resist feelings of sadness, it hangs around forever, periodically erupting inappropriately in our body's attempt to rid itself of that stuff. You must become comfortable with sadness, of your own and others. You must allow the tears and sobs. You will begin to feel good once you accept and acknowledge this expression. Allow yourself to be sad but do not stay there!

When you deny feelings of sadness, it lays dormant where they can do more damage. If you have to cry, then do it! If you have to scream, then do that! Think about the context of your sadness. Sadness is a normal emotion that can make life more interesting. Sadness is often brought on by some form of loss. When we say goodbye to a loved one, we usually feel sad. The sadness is even deeper if a close relationship has ended or a loved one has died. Sadness also helps us appreciate happiness. When our mood eventually changes from sadness toward happiness, the sense of contrast adds to the enjoyment of the mood. Therefore, when you find yourself in a sad state, you must hold that sadness in a high vibration.

Happiness

"Happiness cannot be traveled to, owned, earned, worn or consumed. Happiness is the spiritual experience of living every minute with love, grace, and gratitude." —**Denis Waitley**

Happiness is a state of consciousness that exist within you; it is already there. The more you allow happiness to resonate to you and through you, the more happiness will come into your life! Being happy for no reason is the happiness that you want to experience. The Dalai Lama says *"the purpose of our lives is to be happy."* Often times, one will seek happiness through mediocrity, when happiness should be one's primary goal. It is up to you to choose how you feel. When you make happiness your primary goal instead of a secondary goal, then everything you desire will come with ease and grace. In order to tap fully into your natural state of unlimited happiness, to connect to inner peace and harmony, you must learn how to quiet the mind through meditation and stillness. *"Because I'm happy, clap along If you feel like a room without a roof!" —Pharrell Williams*

Discontent

"Discontent, blaming, complaining, self-pity, cannot serve as a foundation for a good future, no matter how much effort you make." —Eckhart Tolle

If you are not satisfied with your current circumstance, it is because you are longing for an improvement with your life. It is your despairing discontent that yields to the stifling limitations of a poverty stricken consciousness. Are you that disconnected from *Self,* that all your life you have looked at others and really never saw them? When you are content with the mindset of discontent, what you don't want, you get more of. When it comes to discontentment, your experiences originate from circumstances outside of *yourself.* Your discontentment does not serve you.

Peacefulness

"Until he extends his circle of compassion to include all living things, man will not himself find peace." —Albert Schweitzer

Peace is a worthwhile objective—it is security; it is a gift from God. We must learn to be at peace with where we are now! Give gratitude to the Creator in advance, for what is already a manifestation but not delivered in the physical plane. The very center of our being contains the greatest source of love, joy, and peace. The ultimate feeling from anything and everything we dream and desire is peace. The feeling of peace that comes from knowing we are here on purpose. That is the real secret.

Just think of the moment or the last time something resulted in you laughing or when you were in awe at the sound of a song or watching the sunset. In those moments, you were at peace. Once you recognize you have already achieved a state of peace at various moments of your life, and then you should understand that it is possible to be in that state every moment of your life. There is a Divine inner peace and unbounded happiness within you right now!

> *"Within the bosom of man's heart, lies the essence of his peace." —Dawn M. Bunch*

Anxiety

> *"People tend to dwell more on negative things than on good things. So the mind then becomes obsessed with negative things, with judgments, guilt and anxiety produced by thoughts about the future and so on." —Eckhart Tolle*

Anxiety is a scary emotion that will literally overpower one's life, if you allow it! The vast majority of us suffer from this self-inflicting egoic emotion that will send many of us to our graves if we don't learn to control the thoughts and the vibration. This emotion right here sends you indicators that either something bad is going to happen or that something feels off. That is nothing but STRESS to the 10th power!

Beloveds, this is the sort of egoic emotion that will cripple you in mind, body, soul and spirit. It will have you feeling agitated, nervous and worried about events that have not happened. This is the result of false premises that you created within your own consciousness. While this emotion is based on real or imagined events, it will have you in a negative state of mind. And guess what else? It will have a negative impact on your quality of life!

Yes, this emotion makes you feel powerless but when you incorporate pure positive thoughts and meditation into your life, this egoic emotion can no longer ride that wave toward your happiness and well-being. So, when you are in the moment, you become focused on the positive things in life being in that perfect place called *NOW*! Continue to reinforce and affirm daily affirmations. Visualize yourself in that peaceful place and learn to stay there! It's ok if you get knocked off of that peaceful square. The greatest thing about enjoying life is that you know how to get back on it! We are vibrational beings in a vibrational universe! This universe only responds to vibration!

When you send out pure positive energy with good intentions, then you will get it back. When you become open and receptive to the goodness of all that is and embrace it, good things will come to you. "And So It Is!"

Harmonious

"Keep your thoughts and feelings in harmony with your actions. The surest way to realize your purpose is to eliminate any conflict...that exists between what you're thinking and feeling and how you are living your days." — Dr. Wayne W. Dyer

One must possess a quiescent mind to live in a continuous harmonious state! Harmony is the culminating potential of balance. It is superior to the law of nature! When you are in the present moment, you remain in a harmonious state. It is the unwavering and unchanging principle that governs all that is.

Discordance

"Couples are whole and not wholes, what agrees disagrees, the concordant is discordant. From all things one and from one all things." —Heraculitus

Whenever there is discord, there is confusion! Is there harmony in your relationship right now? If you answered no, then you are not in harmony with yourself! If that is the case then whatever experiences that you had in the past, they seemed to have followed you. This is known as karmic emotional luggage full of abuse, fear, low self-esteem, no self-love and no self-worth! Believe it or not, all of this *stuff* is standing in your way! How does one rid themselves of this unwanted luggage? Take control of your destiny by simply cleaning out your luggage. Be accountable for your life and know your purpose! If you are not in harmony with self, you can never be in harmony with anyone or anything.

Therefore, you must be in complete harmony with yourself that which allows you to be in harmony with anyone and anything. The key to your perfect union with your spouse or significant other is to allow that harmonious flow of unconditional love and light into your circle. You and your Twin Flame (Divine Compliment) will discover the joyous and peaceful circle of unconditional love, limitless love, affection, compromising, and faithfulness. But you must release all old *stuff*; by clearing out your luggage the clearing that karmic connection. You will be well on your way on this wondrous journey towards your greater good.

"Though you were part of each other's journey, it was just not meant to be."

"The great teachings unanimously emphasize that all the peace, wisdom, and joy in the universe are already within us; we don't have to gain, develop, or attain them. We're like a child standing in a beautiful park with his eyes shut tight. We don't need to imagine trees, flowers, deer, birds, and sky; we merely need to open our eyes and realize what is already here, who we really are— as soon as we quit pretending we're small or unholy." ~
—Unknown

CHAPTER TWELVE

HEALTH ON THE SAME FREQUENCY
HEALTH ON THE SAME FREQUENCY

*"A healthy body and soul come from an
unencumbered mind and body." Ymber Delecto*

Healthy Pure Positive Thoughts

Healthy thoughts give you quality health, and poor thoughts give you poor health. When you engage in healthy thoughts, and believe that you are abundantly healthy and that every cell in your body heals quickly and with ease, then the universe will grant you that abundance of good health. However, if you engage in sickly thoughts, then the universe will grant an abundance of sickness.

Love Your Temple

Author:

Loving your body will free your soul. This is what I want you to do for your body…Love It…When you love your body, you will discover the powerful secrets to having a body you can love, with a soul freeing experience. You must talk to your body because you love your body. Tell your body that it is abundantly healthy from head to toe and you must think and believe it within every fiber of your being that it is! Tell your body that every cell in it heals quickly and with ease! Accept your body as it is and trust that it will love you back.

Affirmation

I am all that is! I am constantly evolving and expanding because of my love for you.
Hey world, my body is without a doubt the most radiant, strong, beautiful incarnation from GOD.
My body is that which comes from Creation. My body is of beautified physical-ness.

When you vibrate pure positive energy that is what you will attract into your life.

When you communicate and make that connection with your physical-ness. Then and only then will you begin to appreciate your body, and who you really and truly are. Everything else will fall into place!

Once you begin to love who you are, you will be able to set certain goals for yourself to live a better quality of life, and to have total well-being. This means deep cleaning in mind, body, soul, and spirit. The goal here is to develop a loving relationship with your body.

Love yourself as you are! When you have entered into this state of well-being, then you become joyous and at peace with *you*! To love your physical self is to *be* in love with your *physical self*! So, whatever goals that you set for yourself, set them with loving *you* and with good intentions. Set them with self-love and self-worth at the top of your list of goals. This process consists of revamping your entire consciousness mentally, physically and spiritually through that deep cleansing. They say out with the old...In with the new diet.

The most important thing that you can do for your body is to LOVE IT, ADORE IT, EMBRACE IT, FEEL IT, SEE IT, APPRECIATE IT, ACCEPT IT, and be ACCOUNTABLE for IT. When you LOVE, LOVE, LOVE your body, beautiful things will begin to take place. You will become healthier, vibrant and rejuvenated. Your vibration will attract those of a vibrational match into your circle. Always be mindful that your body is your TEMPLE filled with great sacredness! You must love and treat your body it like a temple! When you give your body the purified goodness of love, your body becomes an all-embracing fullness of beauty.

What Diet Are You On?

What is it that YOU are feeding your body? Is it healthy, unhealthy or a little bit of both? Let's break it down and simplify it for you! Pay close attention to the illustration on the next page, and while you're at it, grab something to write with and a note pad! Draw your own chart and work from there! Please keep in mind that this is a process. We want you to be on the path from regression to progression of living a life of happiness and well-being. Can we agree on this?

You are not just preparing yourself for the meeting of your Twin Flame or restoring what is lacking in your relationship or union, but the meeting of the NEW YOU, the advanced announcement of who you will become.

The illustration chart 1-4 on page 134 will help you identify what it is that you must work on when loving your body *(temple),* to become tuned in, tapped in, and turned on. Well, are you on the left or the right? Because you see, there is NO in-between! For those who are on the left, and still feel off, there may be someone or something in your union, causing discord. In this case, it just is not meant to be.

For those riding on the right, well it's obvious that you have no love and regard for your temple. So this means you will have no regard for anyone else, let alone your Twin Flame or significant other. It's okay—we're all here to learn.

The bottom line is that you have to get *YOU* right, before you can be right with someone else. Don't take my word for it, do the work for your mind, body, soul, and spirit. ***When you vibrate pure positive energy that is what you will attract into your life.*** Why not feed your temple the sustenance needed to grow and evolve into the healthy, co-creative, radiant *being* that you were created to be. What sayeth you?

Illustration Chart 1-4

HEALTHY	UNHEALTHY
Healthy Diet: Good Eating Habits	Unhealthy Diet: Poor eating Habits
Internal and External Cleansing	No Cleansing
Healthy Routine Check-ups	Have not had a Routine Check-up in years
Exercise Daily	No exercise
Non-Smoker	Smoker
Healthy Relationship with Self and Others	Unhealthy Relationship with Self and Others

So Beloveds, this area is the most significant piece of your Twin Flame union or relationship. The temples of both avatars must be in sequential alignment with mind, body, soul, and spirit. As you constantly expand and evolve toward your greater good, you become part of the ascension process. Together you create and rebuild the internal and external physical-ness of your physical incarnation.

Author:

"Curtis and I love, respect and feed the most sacred part of our existence; our bodies...our temples. We have mutual respect for one another's temple and passion for great health and well-being. There is no jealousy, envy, nor is there any insecurity of whose temple is and looks better. Why? It's simple with Twin Flames, we are the same, and we are mirrored. When I look at him, I see myself! When he looks at me, he sees himself! But together, we see one!

Within your perfect union lies a passion for the love, honor and beauty of one's body (temple). Often times we disregard and ignore the many vibrational indicators that our bodies send us. Just think of the all the times that we ignored those indicators that have resulted in the progression of a dis-eased, dis-harmonized and unbalanced physical state of being.

Okay, what is being said here is that because you continue to ignore those vibrational indicators, you have adopted a physical, mental and emotional imbalance. Only now, you have acquired some

Dehydration is very prevalent among humans today. People are just not putting enough water into their bodies.

sort of ailment within the physical constraints of the internal and external structure of your body. Yes, the body ages and deteriorates as it continues to go through the process of life's evolutionary cycle… it is and it does! But, why help the process?

Let's say that you can alter your DNA to regenerate new cells every minute and slow down the aging process, giving your body longevity allowing the mind, body, soul, and spirit to heal itself. Would you be willing to slow it down?

Keep in mind that only *YOU* possess the power to do so, unless you are an alien! Yes, there is a such consciousness that goes far beyond our human hybrid comprehension and understanding. It is the knowing of that (space——, time ◯, and time-space—— ◯ reality), which we live in now. That is another book of course…

Loving Our Bodies with the Goodness of Water

Author:

"One of the most important elements that we love our bodies with is…

…ALKALINE

…WATER Ph 6 - 7.5

We are sticklers when it comes to *hydration!*"
Dehydration is very prevalent among humans today. People are just not putting enough water into their bodies. When the body is deprived of *water*…this natural free flowing abundant source, you limit the growth and expansion of the physical part of you. There are people in certain parts of the world that would embrace a drink of water! A source that we take for granted! What happens to a plant if

you do not water it? Well the same thing applies to *YOU*...your body temple! You ***must*** feed your body eight/eight ounce glasses of water or equivalent to half your body weight every day!

DRINK WATER BELOVEDS...

What Are You Feeding Your Bodies?

Feed It Loving Thoughts, Not Toxic Ones!

Whether you are in a union, seeking your Twin Flame or single, know the worthiness of your ***Being!*** Give your body all the love it needs! It is your self-love and self-worth that speaks to your body; with your body; from your body; about your body. When you display all this love for your body, your twin or your other half will do the same. You will be on the same page when it comes to loving your bodies... your temples.

STOP FEEDING your body thoughtless toxins. You are what you think about all day long—thoughts become things. Toxic thoughts create a toxic body! Remember this is when the cleansing diet of the inner self begins. It is the deep cleansing of the mind, body, soul, and spirit—ridding yourself of all the toxic negative Karma lying dormant since your creation. It is absolutely imperative that within this union, you, your Twin or your significant other *must* begin the cleansing process. And yes, it is a **process**!

This is how the Bunch's do it!

We are hydrated because we love our bodies!

When you love your body—it loves you back!

CLEANSE! CLEANSE! CLEANSE!

It is the organs like your liver, your kidneys, your colon, and your lymph system that needs to be cleansed. With all the toxins and heavy metals in your body these organs are being over-worked. A good way to start our cleansing process was to use some baking soda and lemon water.

Wheat Grass/ ChlorOxygen Chlorophyll Concentrate (Alcohol Free)

It's the blood that needs cleansing. It's your cells that need cleansing, it's your digestive tract that needs cleansing, and more importantly, the colon that needs cleansing because that is where all the toxins settle. And get this! When your organs are full of toxins, they are being over-worked and not releasing these toxins from your bodies fast enough.

We cleanse and detox by drinking water with a P H level of 6-7.5, Juicing and Tea Infusions

We juice with fresh beets, carrots, celery, ginger, apples and a garlic cloves using the Ninja Kitchen System. Bottoms up, to the vitamins and minerals all blended together right into your glass with a boost of energy! Wheat Grass Extractor for juicing Wheat Grass. The Benefits of Wheat Grass is sensational! Especially for Women!

Tea Infusions to cleanse the blood, liver, lungs and kidneys with Dandelion Root, Hyssop, Lung Wart, Milk Thistle Seed, Parsley Leaf, Pau de Arco, Red Sage, Sassafras and Yellow Dock Root.

Tea infuses the precious commodity of water with plants that have transmuted the elements of sunshine and earth into nourishing constituents. It is quickly absorbed into the body, inexpensive, and easy to prepare, and its physiological interaction with the body has been proven time again in scientific studies.

Plant food and herbal medicine help in another ways as well: by providing nutrients that are essential to life. Teas are rich in antioxidants called polyphenols which are plant chemicals that may help prevent cancer, heart disease, and other diseases."

-- Monica Myklebust, MD

Our Super Seeds

Raw Hemp Seeds
Raw Pumpkin Seeds
Raw Almonds
Raw Sesame Seeds
Walnuts
Hazelnut
Chia Seeds

Our favorites are Hemp Seed Powder, Raw Hemp Seed, Raw Sesame Seed (good for Migraine Headaches), Chia Seeds (high in protein and omega 3). Our most favorable is Flaxseed and Flaxseed Meal. It prevents heart disease, lowers high cholesterol, helps with weight loss, prevents diabetes, prevents high blood sugar levels, helps to decrease inflammation, promotes intestinal health and helps with constipation and or Diarrhea. Omega 3 Flax is a Brain Food that Decreased +Gets rid of Hot Flashes, Improve Skin Health + Get Rid of Eczema, Dry skin and Acne. It reduces the Risk of Cancer and will boost your Immune System. Maca Root Powder or Tincture improves sexual function and libido so for you men, no need for Viagra. As for women, it is used to alleviate the symptoms of menopause, such as hot flashes and mood swings. Oh but don't take our word for it, do your own due diligence!

Fitness and Exercise

We give our temples daily fitness and exercise to prosper in health as our souls prosper. People often wonder how the Bunch's do it! How do we maintain our bodies to be in such perfect shape? It's is because as Twin Flames, we had to elevate our awareness to become enlightened and awakened to this conscious truth. We see, feel and think very similar patterns of living a life of health, happiness and well-being. We pretty much mirror each other in many things that we do and experience.

Please keep in mind that this book is for informational purposes only and does not in any way give medical advice. Always check with your physician or HMD before you start any diet or exercise programs.

Now that we have shared our story of this perfect union, we hope that the information given to you will assist you in seeking, having and maintain happiness and well-being within your perfect union.

Love, Peace and Riches Blessing Beloveds!

CHAPTER THIRTEEN

POSITIVE LOVE AFFIRMATIONS

Our Unconditional Love is never uncertain. We will love together, pray together, meditate together, laugh together, cry together, play together, eat together, be healthy together...Sharing one soul together...

Before I can meet my Twin Flame, I must first have an unconditional loving relationship with my mind, body and soul and God Source.

An awakened mind, body, soul, and spirit creates a marriage with my higher consciousness and timelessness.

I will embrace and evoke the I AM Presence within ME, having the ultimate love relationship with Self.

I am in love with my true crystalline authentic Self.

I am grateful for the love that I *already* have.

We are Divine Compliments in harmony with love, balance, and *Oneness* of mind, body, soul, and spirit.

When we love unconditionally, we heal our life.

We are the ultimate balancing of the
two primal forces of creation.

Our Twin Flame Union is essential in bringing the
healing of separation into the full vibration of oneness.

Only my Twin Flame pulls out all the negative
Karma deep-rooted inside me.

Together we are the illumination…of the Highest Light.

Our connection of intimacy comes from the
soul and not from the physical plane.

Our souls make *One*, as we are constantly dancing together
to the intimate harmonious beat of Lovemaking.

Our Twin Flameship is a divine marriage of the soul
and nothing can destroy this union—it is eternal.

There will never be a love more powerful
than our Twin Flame Love.

As Twin Flames, it is our destiny to ascend together.

Our Twin Flame Union is truly our Garden of
Eden; our Heaven right here on Earth.

Our Twin Flame Union was designed for a spiritual mission
and incarnated to work and be together with a purpose.

Together we are complete in mind, body, soul, and spirit.

We are two Christ conscious beings joined as one.

The "I Am," is ever and fully present in the both of us.

We have a divine connectedness, unconditional
love and mutual respect for each other.

Within our perfect Twin Flame Union lies a passion for
the love, honor and beauty of our body *(temple)*.

Loving our body will free our soul.

Together we are abundantly healthy in
mind, body, soul and spirit.

We have the perfect Love and the perfect Union.

Our chemistry creates an almighty vortex through which
Divine Love flows, as it anchors onto the Earth plane.

We worship the creative God and Goddess in each other.

We affirm our love and gratitude for *Self,* all
beings, and our Twin Flame relationship.

When we are apart, we join in conscious Love
Making through our heart chakras.

Our Sacral Chakras are healed, cleansed and open.

We expand and evolve into the manifestation of a
divine soul union through our own collective good. We
possess a healthy and harmonious Twin Flameship.

Affirming together with your Twin Flame or alone you open your heart to love; you are opening up the communication channels between you and your Twin Flame. These are the indicators through this divine soul union putting you on the path to ascension.

DON'T TAKE MY WORD FOR IT!
DON'T TAKE MY WORD FOR IT!

References from other sources

Have you ever dreamt of finding that perfect love? Believe that there is someone created for you in this physical realm that can satisfy the intense longing you often feel for love, happiness and fulfilment? Find out how you can be drawn closer to your perfect love, your Twin Flame.

THE TWIN FLAME EXPERIENCE

There is a harmonious flow of unconditional love that is present from the very beginning of this connection. It is through the Creative Source which flows through your Twin flame connection. Twin Flames have always been connected to each other since the day of their creation. As they become united with each other, they are One connected to God Source. When Twin flames join together in harmony and love, they share the same energy.

Twin Flame love is not human love; it is Divine Love. This Divine Compliment uses two human portals to channel their love and light to the planet. Two humans totally united in unconditional love and mutual respect to ALL mankind through the Will of the Creator/ God/Source.

TWIN FLAME AND DIVINE TIME

Twin Flames will present themselves when the *moment* is right. You must look beyond the ego and the physical limitations that may exist between you and your Twin at the time of meeting. You will both be driven to work together in some form to become the best and highest manifestation of your soul here on this Earthly plane. The connection to your Twin flame will happen at the apropos time when you consciously surrender to the calling and allow this divine connection to come in.

Twin Flames

The third dimension is often referred to as 'In The Box'. When your polarities merge, your male and female aspects will move 'Out of the Box' igniting and creating union with your Twin Flame or Twin Aspect. As consciousness moves toward reunion, people miss their twin soul aspect and feel incomplete, often abandoned, lost, and depressed. They cannot find themselves. A piece of them is always missing. They search for it in third dimension but never completely find it.

If they are lucky, they <u>find someone</u> who comes close to making them feel whole. They want someone to love them, share with them and help them through this journey. While here, you can meet someone who acts as a catalyst, carrying the frequency of your Twin Flame, giving you the feeling of union, while making love.

Source Referenced: http://www.crystalinks.com/twinflames.
html Ellie

Welcome To Souls In Bloom
Engaging Your Soul For Purposeful Living

Twin Flame Relationship
* Introduction to the Twin Flame Relationship
* Clearing Karmic Ties
* Integration of the Twin Flame Relationship

Introduction to the Twin Flame Relationship

I talk about how to recognize a Twin Flame Relationship, why it is significant at this time of our evolution and what it takes to manifest this level of relationship in the world. I discuss the challenges and the reasons why freedom is an essential base for this relationship in order for the higher purpose of both individuals and this union to become a physical reality.

Clearing Karmic Ties

Our society tends to have a romantic view of what a soul mate is. There are many souls that we have been with before that we could have mated with, but the Twin Flame Relationship is the next step, a match in purpose. Those people that have recognized their Twin Flame in the world usually have gone beyond a romanticized view of life and relationships. Many people can pass by their twin flame on the street and not recognize them, for true recognition comes from the Soul and a knowing of purpose. This fails to be a knowing from intellect; rather, it is a knowing that comes from a deeper place within our heart's flame.

Romanticized love looks at the world from an outer personality perspective and operates more from a collective Idealized concept of love based on meeting each other's needs.

When we are connected to our purpose we can recognize the purpose for relationship. This has nothing to do with how a person acts towards us. If we are concerned so much about how a person acts towards us, then <u>the relationship</u> is all about our own ideals or wishful thinking rather than a higher purpose for the relationship that serves in the world. If we are truly coming from our hearts with a sincere desire to evolve in relationships, then we will have impact on those people that are in resonance with us.

As I, a woman on the path of service, take action in the physical world from the blueprint within my heart's flame, I create an opening for my twin flame to easily access the blue print within his heart's flame that compliments mine.

True love comes from the Soul connection and sees not only the positive but also the negative aspects of <u>the relationship</u> and is able to acquire the tools from spirit in order to transform it to fulfill a higher purpose. Where there is a resonance in purpose, there will be impact because the Soul is then in command of the outer world, aligning those people whose pieces of the cosmic puzzle fit. There are karmic ties in all relationships because we are all in a place of evolution and we have a history.

The Twin Flame Relationship isn't any different. All we can do is clear our own part in any negative behavior patterns and resonant energies within <u>the relationship</u> that may interfere with the growth of the relationship and the highest evolution of our Twin Flame.

We are not responsible for anybody else's spiritual growth. We cannot do the spiritual work for our Twin Flame. We can only engage in the relationship at the level that it is occurring. As we clear our karmic ties, the history of discord in our etheric records is transmuted. This frees up the energy for the Soul to create the space in the physical world that allows the relationship to be in present time aligned in service. This vibration goes out to our Twin Flame wherever they are on the planet and they are able to act in accordance with the intent of the Twin Soul Alliance.

Integration of the Twin Flame Relationship

The number one reason why so many relationships split up is because there is a lack of alignment with the Soul and the Higher Purpose for <u>the relationship</u>. This means coming into balance with the male and female principles of life within us.

This is going to look different for a man than it does for a woman. If a man or woman is still coming from his or her ego looking for that gratification, nurturance or protection from their partner, then we have the circumstances that we have in the world with people that change relationships like they change their socks. When one or the other person is unable to fulfill the other's needs, then the relationship ends.

In order to integrate the Twin Flame Relationship, we have to integrate and follow our own Soul and Higher Purpose in life. If either person lacks an alignment with their Soul and higher purpose then the outer manifestation goes to a lower vibration, creating enmeshed relationship. When we have the balance of the male and female principles of life within we have an alignment with our Souls purpose. This means we have our inner self in harmony with our outer self, our higher mind with our heart, and we create a new world.

In these classes, we integrate the information from our Future Self and the Future Twin Flame Relationship that is living this relationship in the physical world. We practice the disciplines necessary to achieve the Ultimate Relationship with our Self and the tools necessary to awaken the Twin Flame Relationship in the physical reality.

Linda Sajiw began her path of spiritual awakening in the early 1980s when she studied the Kabbalah, the spiritual and meditation practices of various eastern religions, dream analysis and hypnosis. Her degree comes from the University of Life following her inner guidance to align with her God-essence.

Some of her friends and coworkers thought her a bit eccentric. While they were out getting high, she was learning about various psychological disorders and addiction in abusive relationships. She was discovering recurring threads linking early childhood development with similarities in behavioral patterns later in life.

Along with her spirit-guided studies, Linda has had a 12-year career as a professional visual artist whereby she learned that creating true art involves more than just the techniques of making pretty pictures. She learned that her inner self was in conflict with her outer self, causing her to experience a lot of fragmentation and collapses in her physical world.

In the early spring of 1990, she had a conscious expanding experience that gave her a broader sense of knowing her Self as an Infinite Creator Being in a vast universe every bit as brilliant as the stars in the sky. Everything cracked open in her life. She discovered that she had been holding together a role-based identity with a construct of fear derived from creating safety in an early chaotic home environment and fitting into the school system. It was like having an 80-watt light bulb put into a 40-watt body socket. In connecting with her Infinite Presence, all her limiting concepts were shattered, affecting her brain synapses, thought and body processes. She discovered that her soul's vision was very different from her limiting egos, and set forth to come into full resonance with that vision.

She learned to see through the lens of her multidimensional self. Now she discerns almost completely from her feeling, intuitive sense rather than just external sight. She has developed a conscious awareness of soul-to-soul communication in relationship, resulting from her 15 years of working with energy and her treks in nature, "talking with the trees", and "listening to the voices in the wind". She specializes in tracking and transforming fear patterning in the mental, emotional, physical and spiritual bodies.

Having reconnected with some abilities from other lifetime selves, she shares a unique perspective in consciousness using her poetry and workshop events to create a sacred space for you to light up the wholeness of your Being. She presents an avenue for you to discover your piece of the Divine Plan and the tools to bring it forward.

Same Gender Twin Flame Relationships

Although there is not a whole lot of information available in books or on the web regarding same sex Twin Flames. It just so happens that male/male and female/female are in relationships not by chance but by Spiritual design. We needn't judge it! Spirit is not adhered to the physical gender. Spiritual is non-physical—it is mere energy. So in a sense; souls have feminine and masculine energy, there is no sexual gender within the spiritual world. Same gender Twin Flames have reunited within the physical plane of this universe just as female/male have. This incarnation can be in both men and women physical bodies.

If Twin Flames are incarnating into physical three dimensional bodies in time/space reality, they can incarnate into two bodies of the same gender. One will have a more dominant masculine or feminine energy and the other will have the exact opposite. It is certainly possible for this incarnation to enter this physical plane as one gender or the other.

Whatever your sexual orientation is, no matter what the gender is everyone has a Twin Flame and will be drawn to them. You must be willing, open, and receptive to your spiritual truth. All you are really doing is meeting your true authentic crystalline self—the other you. So whether your other half is male, or female, Twin Flame reunions are about unconditional love. Twin Flames are reuniting to demonstrate unconditional love and mutual respect to all man-kind. There is a wave of same gender Twin Flames here to demonstrate that it is not just about the physical attraction. Moreover, Twin Flame reunions are happening on the spiritual plane. It does not matter if their physical bodies are of the same gender.

Noted...One's physical gender or sexual preference has nothing to do with their bi-gender balance and being drawn to their Twin Flame. Their pairing may be of the same gender. But on the contrary, when we hear about relationships that are of lesbian, gay, transsexual, transgender, or same sex marriages, we have a tendency to lean to our own understanding...A stereotypical consciousness based on the gender roles of today's society. Has it ever occurred that they have met their Twin Flame on the spiritual and soul level?

As it states...Spirit has no sexual gender... We all are here to spread unconditional love and to embrace our journey toward ascension.

Twin Flames

THE INFINITY OF TWIN FLAMES IN PERFECT HARMONY

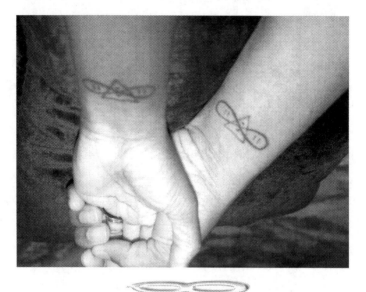

"We are the I AM Presence of infinity...We are Twin Flames as the Divine 11:11 is our beacon.
Our souls are of the feminine in 11 and the Masculine in 22 created together...Sharing the same
energy...We are constantly expanding, channeling through the Twin Flame love portal.
Together we ascend to the top of the divine triangle reaching PERFECT HARMONY in 33...
IT IS OUR ETERNAL DESTINY...AND SO IT IS..."

*Twin Flames are ultimate soul mates who are already paired in the
Higher Realm. *Twin Flames experience their last lifetime here on earth
together. Twin Flames love mutually, unconditionally and without limits.
Twin Flames have no doubt of who they are and that they are meant to be*

together. Twin Flames are the ultimate <u>*power*</u> *couple and are powerful. The energy between Twin Flames is so intense that it is unlikely that both will not feel it. The attraction between them is too strong to deny and keeps them BOTH coming back together. Their time apart is never too long and they are never too far away. Twin Flames share most of each other's strengths and weaknesses, but may experience them differently. Twin Flames are not karmic soulmates. Soulmates are plentiful. A Twin Flame is only one. That means that there can only be one. There is no such thing as 'twin energy' going from one body to another, as a Twin Flames body is already chosen and as it appears above it will be below. BOTH individuals will feel the call, pull, heat, energy, attraction, intensity and love for one another. Twin Flames experience a different level of connection/bonding and love, which can be very intense and magical. Twin Flames are ALREADY paired above and it is the goal to make it so below. There cannot be two Twin Flames per one person. There is ONLY one. When Twin Flames are meant to be together, they will be together at the same time on the same plane. Twin Flames are the last 'soul mate' you will ever have on this earth, meaning this IS your last lifetime here on earth…meaning all your lessons and karmic relationships are up (or are needed to be taken care of asap), and it is now time to move to a higher level of existence.*

Twin Flames experience life quite differently than most. And are so much more than what people believe a Twin Flame is. The term Twin Flame that is being used now does not do the actual meaning of who we are justice. This may be so because that is not what we are truly called. Many are using their own definitions to keep from accepting the fact that: A. They do not have a Twin Flame, at least that exist on this earth at this time, or B. The person they thought was their Twin Flame is not.

Twin Flame unions are those created by Universe/God at a time when there are no more lessons to be learned for those individuals. This means that for everything they have done on this planet they can now relax and have whatever they so desire. Again, this means that they are of a higher spirituality than most and have not only been gifted great knowledge, but can now live free from restraint in all areas of life. Twin Flames are awakened for the purpose of helping hundreds, thousands, and possibly millions find their way in this world, and have knowledge in all areas of life because of the many lifetimes they have lived. This is the truest form of love that will ever be. There is not one person in this world who will be able to take the place of a Twin Flame. Twin Flames are to be together, and if on this earth, and great lengths will be taken with the help of Universe to see that happen. Twin Flames are rare and can only be accessed by those who are on the spiritual level required for this type of love. It is my thought that every person carries a piece of information, different from others, but vital still the same.

It is my thought that every person carries a piece of information, different from others, vital still the same. This goes for 'experts' too. As a Twin Flame Guru, I have been given information from Source that matches that of other experts, but also KEY pieces of information that is unique to only me. Having had the time to listen to Source-taking in all lessons, information and insight, I am now able to share with you some things that you may not know yet about your own relationship, yourself and your path. We all have a purpose. Finding the other half to your soul is one of the closest you will ever come to figuring out just what that purpose is.

—Llady Sorcha

Source Reference: http://www.lladysorcha.com/twin-flames/

THE SMOOTHIE FIX
THE SMOOTHIE FIX

Come join us in shifting your consciousness to a higher state and making a commitment to change your life style. If you desire to live a life of happiness and well-being, and a quality of life—change starts *NOW!*

Here are a few Smoothie Recipes! Remember, you are what you eat!

Oatmeal with the Quickness for Breakfast:
1c Organic Rolled Oats
½ Banana cut up fresh
¼ c Strawberries fresh or frozen
1c Home Made Almond Milk
1tblsp Raw Agave
1 c Filtered Water Alkaline of 6-7.5
Blend! Walla! ☺

Anytime Berry Blast Smoothie:
½ c-Filtered Water Alkaline of 6-7.5
4 Ice Cubes
½ c Organic Almond Milk
¼ c Blueberries fresh or frozen
¼ c Strawberries fresh or frozen

cont.

¼ c Blackberries fresh or frozen

¼ c Raspberries fresh or frozen

1tspn Raw Agave

1 tsp. Organic Peanut Butter

¼ c Walnuts

¼ c Raw Pumpkin Seed

1 tbsp. Chia Seeds

1 tbsp. Dark Flaxseed

Blend! Walla ☺

The Orange Blossom

½ c-Filtered Water Alkaline of 6-7.5

4 Ice Cubes

2 Clementine or Navel Oranges fresh

1 Vanilla Bean or ¼ tsp. of Pure Vanilla Extract

½ c Raspberries fresh or frozen

1 tsp. of Fresh Ginger Root

½ c Greek Vanilla Yogurt Organic

1tspn Raw Agave

Blend! Walla ☺

The BYBP Juice
(Better Your Blood Pressure)

1 small red organic Beetroot, peeled and sliced

2 red organic Apples, peeled cored and sliced

3 organic Celery stalks

Put into your juicer!

Walla!

Juicing should become part of your daily diet.

Note: Want healthy Blood Pressure and keep it low; take all three non-GMO natural supplements:

Pure Ceylon cinnamon

Magnesium Malate

Vitamin B6

How about those **GREENS**!

Organic Veggie Vitality

½ c-Filtered Water Alkaline of 6-7.5

½ c Dandelion (fresh) chopped

½ c Baby Spinach

½ c Kale chopped

½ c Green Leaf Lettuce

2 Asparagus chopped

4 oz. Wheat Grass (juiced) or 1 scope if using Powder

2 Garlic Cloves

1 tsp. of Fresh Ginger Root

1 Radish chopped

1 tbsp. Chopped Walnuts

1 tbsp. Raw Pumpkin Seeds

1 tbsp. Raw Sunflower Seeds

1 tbsp. Raw Sesame Seeds

Pinch of Cayenne Pepper

Blend! Walla ☺

These are a few smoothie recipes from my next book "THE HEALING CABINET" coming out this summer 2016.

You should always consult an HHP (Holistic Health Care Provider, Physician, or health care practitioner *before taking any supplements as they may interfere with certain medications.*

FORGIVENESS WILL BRING GOODNESS

There is no ascension, there is no expansion and there is no growth toward your greater good without forgiveness. The Law of forgiveness works with the energy of allowing-ness, and seeing all as LOVE. It is the Non-violence that is the natural outgrowth of the law of forgiveness and love. All good comes from forgiveness. It is a truth that the co-creation of the human species is due to man forgiving and being forgiven. Forgiveness is holiness. The universe is held together by forgiveness. Forgiveness is the might of the mighty; forgiveness is quiet of mind. Forgiveness and peacefulness are qualities of a harmonious flow of LOVE, that which represents eternal virtue.

"When you begin to believe in the power of this universe, things will become evident that your Mind, Body, Soul and Spirit will be in that place of blissfulness and completeness."

—*Dawn M. Bunch*

ABOUT THE AUTHOR
ABOUT THE AUTHOR

I am in acknowledgement that I am a spark of God!

Dawn Bunch is a non-fiction author, writer and spiritual motivator who is not aligned with any particular religion or tradition. Her first book Notes From Women of Timelessness was self-published with Barnes and Nobles.com and Amazon.com. *Mirror Image* reveals the vision of true divine, eternal unconditional Twin Flame love. Dawn allows her spiritual intuitiveness to guide her while traveling on the path of ascension to fulfill her mission giving love and enlightenment to humanity and the world.

Her message is of Love, Empowerment, Self-Help, Motivation, Inspiration, and Liberation. Not only will her books help enhance the readers' consciousness; they will raise the readers' awareness level to help them identify who they are, make them feel good about who they are and help them identify their life's purpose as she has identified her purposeful journey toward her greatness to be.

In her writings, she conveys a simple yet profound message of clarity and steps to improve your way of life, by connecting with your higher self, through meditation, prayer, affirmations, chakra cleansing and healing. Dawn's intentions are to help those to become awakened and seek transformation in their lives. Her sole mission as the Spiritual Yielding Twin is to raise the consciousness of humanity.

Dawn Bunch helps you to discover your piece of the Divine Plan. This nurturing tool allows this plan to emerge from the depths of your *being*—tapping into that inner power only to find true love and happiness that only lies within your soul. Then and only then are you able to share it with the world.

Dawn Bunch lives in Delaware with her husband Curtis and their daughter Curstan. She has and eldest daughter Andrea and her two children Asiraah and Yasir who live in New Jersey.

NOTES
NOTES

1. Zollie Harris
2. Dr. Wayne W. Dyer
3. James 1:17 KJV Bible
4. Abraham Hicks
5. Job 23:10
6. Curtis J. Bunch
7. Matthew 19: 5, 6
8. Sourced Referenced: http://www. twinflamesinlove.com Rev. Shaneetha Akinlana the Love Doctor
9. Source Referenced: http://www.kelleyrosano.com Author Kelley Rosano
10. 3 John 1:2 (NKJV)
11. Dawn M. Bunch
12. Dawn M. Bunch
13. Dawn M. Bunch
14. Dawn M. Bunch
15. Deepak Chopra
16. Jim Rohn
17. Denis Waitley
18. Pharell Williams
19. Eckhart Tolle
20. Albert Schweitzer

21. Dawn Bunch
22. Eckhart Tolle
23. Dr. Wayne W. Dyer
24. Heraclitus
25. Unknown
26. Ymber Delecto
27. Monica Myklebust, MD
28. http://www.crystallinks.com Ellie
29. Sourced Referenced http://www.soulsinbloom.com/main.
    htm Linda Sajiw Welcome to Souls in Bloom
30. Sourced Referenced: http://www.lladysorcha.com
    twin-flames/
31. Dawn Bunch

If you have questions, comments, or if you would like
more information about Twin Flame Relationships,
please visit www.askdawnbunch.com

"Within the twelve dimensional space of consciousness, we are mirrored—we are Twin Flames—we are divine compliment."
                                        —*Dawn M. Bunch*

Printed in the United States
By Bookmasters